THE CONTEMPORARY SHAKESPEARE

Edited by A. L. Rowse

Henry V

Modern Text with Introduction

UNIVERSITY PRESS OF AMERICA

University Press of America,® Inc.

4720 Boston Way
Lanham, MD 20706

3 Henrietta Street
London WC2E 8LU England

Distributed to the trade by The Scribner Book Companies

Library of Congress Cataloging in Publication Data

Shakespeare, William, 1564-1616.
  Henry V.

  (The Contemporary Shakespeare)
  1. Henry V, King of England, 1337-1422 — Drama.
I. Rowse, A. L. (Alfred Leslie), 1903-   . II. Title.
III. Series: Shakespeare, William, 1564-1616. Plays
(University Press of America : Pbk. ed.)
PR2812.A2R64   1985   822.3'3   85-680
ISBN 0-8191-3918-1 (pbk.)

This play is also available as part of Volume III in a seven volume
clothbound and slipcased set.

Book design by Leon Bolognese

WHY A CONTEMPORARY SHAKESPEARE?

The starting point of my project was when I learned both from television and in education, that Shakespeare is being increasingly dropped in schools and colleges because of the difficulty of the language. In some cases, I gather, they are given just a synopsis of the play, then the teacher or professor embroiders from his notes.

This is deplorable. We do not want Shakespeare progressively dropped because of superfluous difficulties that can be removed, skilfully, conservatively, keeping to every line of the text. Nor must we look at the question statically, for this state of affairs will worsen as time goes on and we get further away from the language of 400 years ago—difficult enough in all conscience now.

We must begin by ridding our mind of prejudice, i.e. we must not pre-judge the matter. A friend of mine on New York radio said that he was 'appalled' at the very idea; but when he heard my exposition of what was proposed he found it reasonable and convincing.

Just remember, I do not need it myself: *I live in the Elizabethan age*, Shakespeare's time, and have done for years, and am familiar with its language, and his. But even for me there are still difficulties—still more for modern people, whom I am out to help.

Who, precisely?

Not only students at school and in college, but all readers of Shakespeare. Not only those, but all viewers of the plays, in the theatre, on radio and television—actors too, who increasingly find pronunciation of the words difficult, particularly obsolete ones—and there are many, besides the difficulty of accentuation.

The difficulties are naturally far greater for non-English-speaking peoples. We must remember that he is our greatest asset, and that other peoples use him a great deal in learning our language. There are no Iron Curtains for him—though, during Mao's Cultural Revolution in China, he was prohibited. Now that the ban has been lifted, I learn that the Chinese in thousands flock to his plays.

Now, a good deal that was grammatical four hundred years ago is positively ungrammatical today. We might begin by removing what is no longer good grammar.

For example: plural subjects with a verb in the singular:

'*Is* Bushy, Green and the earl of Wiltshire dead?' Any objection to replacing 'is' correctly by 'are'? Certainly not. I notice that some modern editions already correct—

These high wild hills and rough uneven ways
Draw*s* out our miles and make*s* them wearisome

to 'draw' and 'make', quite sensibly. Then, why not go further and regularise this Elizabethan usage to modern, consistently throughout?

Similarly with archaic double negatives—'Nor shall you not think neither'—and double comparatives: 'this is more worser than before.' There are hundreds of instances of what is now just bad grammar to begin with.

There must be a few thousand instances of superfluous subjunctives to reduce to simplicity and sense. Today we use the subjunctive occasionally after 'if', when we say 'if it be'. But we mostly say today 'if it is'. Now Shakespeare has hundreds of subjunctives, not only after if, but after though, although, unless, lest, whether, until, till, etc.

I see no point whatever in retaining them. They only add superfluous trouble in learning English, when the great appeal of our language as a world-language is precisely that it has less grammar to learn than almost any. Russian is unbelievably complicated. Inflected languages—German is like Latin in this respect—are really rather backward; it has been a great recommendation that English has been more progressive in this respect in simplifying itself.

Now we can go further along this line: keep a few subjunctives, if you must, but reduce them to a minimum.

Let us come to the verb. It is a great recommendation to modern English that our verbs are comparatively simple to conjugate — unlike even French, for example. In the Elizabethan age there was a great deal more of it, and some of it inconsistent in modern usage. Take Shakespeare's,

'Where is thy husband now? Where be thy brothers?'

Nothing is lost by rendering this as we should today:

Where is your husband now? Where are your brothers?

And so on.

The second and third person singular—all those shouldsts and wouldsts, wilts and shalts, haths and doths, have become completely obsolete. Here a vast simplification may be effected—with no loss as far as I can see, and with advantages from several points of view.

For example, 'st' at the end of a word is rather difficult to say, and more difficult even for us when it is succeeded by a word beginning with 'th'. Try saying, 'Why usurpedst thou this?' Foreigners have the greatest difficulty in pronouncing our 'th' anyway—many never succeed in getting it round their tongues. Many of these tongue-twisters even for us proliferate in Shakespeare, and I see no objection to getting rid of *superfluous* difficulties. Much easier for people to say, 'Why did you usurp this?'—the same number of syllables too.

This pre-supposes getting rid of almost all thous and thees and thines. I have no objection to keeping a few here and there, if needed for a rhyme—even then they are sometimes not necessary.

Some words in Shakespeare have changed their meaning into the exact opposite: we ought to remove that stumbling-block. When Hamlet says, 'By heaven, I'll make a ghost of him that *lets* me', he means *stops*; and we should replace it by stops, or holds me. Shakespeare regularly uses the word 'owe' where we should say own: the meaning has changed. Take a line like, 'Thou dost here usurp the name thou ow'st not': we should say, 'You do here usurp the name you own not', with the bonus of getting rid of two ugly 'sts'.

The word 'presently' in the Elizabethan age did not mean in a few minutes or so, but immediately—instantly has the same number of syllables. 'Prevent' then had its Latin meaning, to go before, or forestall. Shakespeare frequently uses the word 'still' for always or ever.

Let us take the case of many archaic forms of words, simple one-syllable words that can be replaced without the slightest difference to the scansion: 'sith' for since, 'wrack' for wreck, 'holp' for helped, 'writ' for wrote, 'brake' for broke, 'spake' for spoke, 'bare' for bore, etc.

These give no trouble, nor do a lot of other words that he uses: 'repeal' for recall, 'reproof' for disproof, 'decline' for incline. A few words do give more trouble. The linguistic scholar, C. T. Onions, notes that it is sometimes difficult to give the precise meaning Shakespeare attaches to the word 'conceit'; it usually means thought, or fancy, or concept. I do not know that it ever has our meaning; actually the word 'conceited' with him means ingenious or fantastic, as 'artificial' with Elizabethans meant artistic or ingenious.

There is a whole class of words that have completely gone out, of which moderns do not know the meaning. I find no harm in replacing the word 'coistrel' by rascal, which is what it means—actually it has much the same sound—or 'coil' by fuss; we find 'accite' for summon, 'indigest' for formless. Hamlet's word 'reechy', for the incestuous kisses of his mother and her brother-in-law, has gone out of use: the nearest word, I suppose, would be reeky, but filthy would be a suitable modern equivalent.

In many cases it is extraordinary how little one would need to change, how conservative one could be. Take Hamlet's famous soliloquy, 'To be or not to be.' I find only two words that moderns would not know the meaning of, and one of those we might guess:

. . .When he himself might his *quietus* make
    With a bare bodkin? Who would *fardels* bear. . .

'Quietus' means put paid; Elizabethans wrote the Latin 'quietus est' at the bottom of a bill that was paid—when it was—to say that it was settled. So that you could replace 'quietus' by settlement, same number of syllables, though not the same accentuation; so I would prefer to use the word acquittance, which has both.

'Fardels' means burdens; I see no objection to rendering, 'Who would burdens bear'—same meaning, same number of syllables, same accent: quite simple. I expect all the ladies to know what a bodkin is: a long pin, or skewer.

Now let us take something really difficult—perhaps the most difficult passage to render in all Shakespeare. It is the virtuoso comic piece describing all the diseases that horseflesh is heir to, in *The Taming of the Shrew*. The horse is Petruchio's. President Reagan tells me that this is the one Shakespearean part that he played—and a very gallant one too. In Britain last year we saw a fine performance of his on horseback in Windsor Park alongside of Queen Elizabeth II—very familiar ground to William Shakespeare and Queen Elizabeth I, as we know from *The Merry Wives of Windsor*.

Here is a headache for us: Petruchio's horse (not President Reagan's steed) was 'possessed with the glanders, and like to mose in the chine; troubled with the lampass, infected with the fashions, full of windgalls, sped with spavins, rayed with the yellows, past cure of the fives, stark spoiled with the staggers, begnawn with the bots; swayed in the back, and shoulder-shotten; near-legged before, and with a half-cheeked bit, and a headstall of sheep's leather', etc.

What on earth are we to make of that? No doubt it raised a laugh with Elizabethans, much more familiarly acquainted with horseflesh than we are; but I doubt if Hollywood was able to produce a nag for Reagan that qualified in all these respects.

Now, even without his horsemanship, we can clear one fence at the outset: 'mose in the chine'. Pages of superfluous commentary have been devoted to that word 'mose'. There was no such Elizabethan word: it was simply a printer's misprint for 'mourn', meaning dripping or running; so it suggests a running sore. You would need to consult the *Oxford English Dictionary*, compiled on historical lines, for some of the words, others like 'glanders' country folk know and we can guess.

So I would suggest a rendering something like this: 'possessed with glanders, and with a running sore in the back; troubled in the gums, and infected in the glands; full of galls in the fetlocks and swollen in the joints; yellow with jaundice, past cure of the strangles; stark spoiled with the staggers, and gnawed by worms; swayed in the back and shoulder put out; near-legged before, and with a half-cheeked bit and headgear of sheep's leather', etc. That at least makes it intelligible.

Oddly enough, one encounters the greatest difficulty with the least important words and phrases, Elizabethan expletives and malapropisms, or salutations like God 'ild you, Godden, for God shield you, Good-even, and so on. 'God's wounds' was Elizabeth I's favourite swearword; it appears frequently enough in Victorian novels as 'Zounds'— I have never heard anyone use it. The word 'Marry!', as in the phrase 'Marry come up!' has similarly gone out, though a very old gentleman at All Souls, Sir Charles Oman, had heard the phrase in the back-streets of Oxford just after the 1914-18 war. 'Whoreson' is frequent on the lips of coarse fellows in Shakespeare: the equivalent in Britain today would be bloody, in America (I suppose) s.o.b.

Relative pronouns, who and which: today we use who for persons, which for things. In Elizabethan times the two were hardly distinguished and were interchangeable. Provokingly Shakespeare used the personal relative 'who' more frequently for impersonal objects, rivers, buildings, towns; and then he no less frequently uses 'which' for persons. This calls out to be regularised for the modern reader.

Other usages are more confusing. The word 'cousin'

was used far more widely by the Elizabethans for their kin: it included nephews, for instance. Thus it is confusing in the English History plays to find a whole lot of nephews—like Richard III's, whom he had made away with in the Tower of London—referred to and addressed as cousins. That needs regularisation today, in the interests of historical accuracy and to get the relationship clear. The word 'niece' was sometimes used of a grandchild—in fact this is the word Shakespeare used in his will for his little grand-daughter Elizabeth, his eventual heiress who ended up as Lady Barnard, leaving money to her poor relations the Hathaways at Stratford. The Latin word *neptis*, from which niece comes also meant grandchild—Shakespeare's grammar-school education at Stratford was in Latin, and this shows you that he often thought of a word in terms of its Latin derivation.

Malapropisms, misuse of words, sometimes mistaking of meanings, are frequent with uneducated people, and sometimes not only with those. Shakespeare transcribed them from lower-class life to raise a laugh, more frequently than any writer for the purpose. They are an endearing feature of the talk of Mistress Quickly, hostess of the Boar's Inn in East Cheapside, and we have no difficulty in making out what she means. But in case some of us do, and for the benefit of non-native English speakers, I propose the correct word in brackets afterwards: 'You have brought her into such a canaries [quandary]. . .and she's as fartuous [virtuous] a civil, modest wife. . .'

Abbreviations: Shakespeare's text is starred—and in my view, marred—by innumerable abbreviations, which not only look ugly on the page but are sometimes difficult to pronounce. It is not easy to pronounce 'is't', or 'in't', or 'on't', and some others: if we cannot get rid of them altogether they should be drastically reduced. Similarly with 'i'th'', 'o'th'', with which the later plays are liberally bespattered, for "in the" or "of the."

We also have a quite unnecessary spattering of apostrophes in practically all editions of the plays—''d' for the past participle, e.g. 'gather'd'. Surely it is much better to regularise the past participle 'ed', e.g. gathered; and when the last syllable is, far less frequently, to be pronounced, then accent it, gatherèd.

This leads into the technical question of scansion, where a practising poet is necessary to get the accents right, to help the reader, and still more the actor. Most people will hardly notice that, very often, the frequent ending of words in 'ion', like reputation, has to be pronounced with two syllables at the end. So I propose to accent this when necessary, e.g. reputatiòn. I have noticed the word 'ocean' as tri-syllabic, so I accent it, to help, oceàn. A number of words which to us are monosyllables were pronounced as two: hour, fire, tired; I sometimes accent or give them a dieresis, either hoùr or fïre. In New England speech words like prayèr, thëre, are apt to be pronounced as two syllables—closer to Elizabethan usage (as with words like gotten) than is modern speech in Britain.

What I notice in practically all editions of Shakespeare's plays is that the editors cannot be relied on to put the accents in the right places. One play edited by a well known Shakespearean editor had, I observed, a dozen accents placed over the wrong syllables. This is understandable, for these people don't write poetry and do not know how to scan. William Shakespeare knew all about scanning, and you need to be both familiar with Elizabethan usage and a practising traditional poet to be able to follow him.

His earlier verse was fairly regular in scansion, mostly iambic pentameter with a great deal of rhyme. As time went on he loosened out, until there are numerous irregular lines—this leaves us much freer in the matter of modernising. Our equivalents should be rhythmically as close as possible, but a strait-jacket need be no part of the equipment. A good Shakespearean scholar tells us, 'there is no necessity for Shakespeare's lines to scan absolutely. He thought of his verse as spoken rather than written and of his rhythmic units in terms of the voice rather than the page.'

There is nothing exclusive or mandatory about my project. We can all read Shakespeare in any edition we like—in the rebarbative olde Englishe spelling of the First Folio, if we wish. Any number of conventional academic editions exist, all weighed down with a burden of notes, many of them superfluous. I propose to make most of them unnecessary—only one occasionally at the foot of very few pages. Let the text be freed of superfluous difficulties, remove obstacles to let it speak for itself, while adhering conservatively to every line.

We really do not need any more editions of the Plays on conventional lines—more than enough of those exist already. But A Contemporary Shakespeare on these lines—both revolutionary and conservative—should be a help to everybody all round the world—though especially for younger people, increasingly with time moving away from the language of 400 years ago.

INTRODUCTION

With *Henry V* in 1599 Shakespeare completed the quartet of English history plays begun with *Richard II* in 1595 and continued with the two parts of *Henry IV* in 1597–8. We should notice the variety, how different these plays are, from the lyricism of *Richard II*, through the mixture of comedy with history in *Henry IV*, to *Henry V* which is different again, with something of a patriotic epic about it. This may not be to everybody's taste today, though it certainly spoke again to the hearts of the generation of 1940 when Britain was in mortal danger. In particular we find the boastful slanging-matches between English and French both naif and tiresome, as simpler Elizabethans did not: they liked that sort of thing.

In the long set speeches of the first Act, in which the claim of Henry V to the French crown (he was more than half-French) is set out at tedious length, Shakespeare is simply versifying as he goes along from the Chronicles, principally Holinshed. And we should notice that he is always better when creating out of his own head. His 'source' he relies on for the framework, the plot, the facts—sometimes wrong, as in blaming the Archbishop of Canterbury for inciting Henry to war (he needed no encouragement). The fun is all Shakespeare's—as Dr. Johnson observed, and Shakespeare corroborates in his portrait of himself as Berowne in *Love's Labour's Lost:* his original bent was all for comedy.

Henry V is enlivened by comic scenes, particularly in the scenes around the Welsh, Irish, and Scots captains, in which Shakespeare caricatured their respective brogues with his usual linguistic virtuosity. Pistol also appears again with his extraordinary lingo—(Shakespeare must have had some particular individual in mind)—a braggart from the wars such as he observed in Elizabethan London. But the most fabulous comic of all, Falstaff, had to be omitted as too outsize. His weight would have broken the bounds of the play; Shakespeare had to change his plan for the very different scheme he had in mind, the depiction of Henry V as the hero-King he was to the Elizabethans and the evocation of the nostalgic memories of Agincourt.

Here again the King in action is not to everybody's taste. Professor Dover Wilson, however, says sympathetically, '*Henry V* is a play which men of action have been wont silently to admire, and literary men—at any rate during the last hundred and thirty years—volubly to contemn.' So much the worse for the literary men, such liberal doctrinaires as Hazlitt, for example: showing no generosity of imagination, still less political or historical understanding.

For Henry is, above all, a political type, an ideal ruler, who rises to the challenge of the tremendous responsibility for other men's lives that the ruler, whether King or President, so bears. And Henry does not bear it lightly: his soul is exposed to us in the wonderful night scene before Agincourt, in which he argues the issue fairly with a common soldier and then lays the matter before God in prayer:

Upon the King! Let us our lives, our souls,
Our debts, our careful wives,
Our children, and our sins, lay on the King!
We must bear all . . .

We have still more reason to appreciate and understand
the dire responsibility resting upon those in ultimate
control, in a nuclear age, of the release of nuclear power.

For a fuller appreciation of Henry V's character and the
political issues I must refer the reader to my longer
Introduction to the play in my *Prefaces to Shakespeare's
Plays*. Here we must concentrate on the drama.

The dramatist met the difficulties of the extended field
of action overseas by a direct appeal to the imagination of
the audience, with a descriptive chorus before each Act.
With his usual courtesy he asks pardon for

> The flat unraisèd spirits that have dared
> On this unworthy scaffold to bring forth
> So great an object. Can this cockpit hold
> The vasty fields of France? Or may we cram
> Within this wooden O the very casques
> That did affright the air at Agincourt?

The wooden O was the Globe Theatre which the Burbages
had erected on the South Bank of the Thames, using the
timbers of the old Theatre in Shoreditch which had given
Shakespeare his earlier opportunities. Henceforth the Globe
was to be the Company's permanent home.

At each appearance as Chorus Shakespeare wooed the
sympathy and applause of the audience. In the Sonnet
which concludes the play as Epilogue we have him in his
own person:

> Thus far, with rough and all-unable pen,
> Our bending author has pursued the story—

and opportunity should always be taken to cast the author
himself as Chorus. He concludes with a reference to his
own *Henry VI* trilogy, the historical sequel, with which he
had first won success:

Which oft our stage has shown.

But what a prodigious development had been registered in his work as a dramatist in those past seven or eight years!

We are given indications of the contemporary scene as always, here in direct references. The long war with Spain was approaching a climax with the quasi-national resistance in Ireland under a great leader, O'Neill. The effort to equip the largest army yet sent across the Irish Channel appears in

> The armourers, accomplishing the knights,
> With busy hammers closing rivets up,
> Give dreadful note of preparatiòn.

The army was under the command of Essex, who was given a grand send-off from the City:

> How London doth pour out her citizens

like 'antique Rome' fetching 'their conquering Caesar in—

> As, by a lower but loving likelihood
> Were now the General of our gracious Empress—
> As in good time he may—from Ireland coming,
> Bringing rebellion broachèd on his sword,
> How many would the peaceful city quit
> To welcome him!

The Irish crisis stoked up the fires of patriotism once more, so much to the fore in this play as in the earlier history plays. We have Irish references in this, not only in Captain MacMorris, but yet again to the Irish kern, riding bare-legged.

For the modern reader the play presents greater linguistic

difficulties than any, and modernisation is more necessary than ever. We have a whole scene in French, in which the Princess Katherine (ancestress of Elizabeth I) is learning English: a good deal of her love-scene with Henry is in French, while French phrases abound. All this is translated, the whole of the first, Act III, Scene 4, in the Appendix, the rest in footnotes or in brackets.

How did Shakespeare come by all this French? Well, about this time he was lodging in the City in Silver Street, with a French family, the Montjoies, who were tire-makers or headdress makers. Shakespeare was on confidential terms with Madame Montjoie, the betrothal of whose daughter he performed on her behalf. The French herald in the play, Montjoy, is given a considerable part, and the reference to people wearing their own hair pinpoints the association. No doubt Shakespeare received help from that quarter.

The respective brogues of the Welsh, Irish and Scotch captains has been rendered less outlandish than the original, leaving enough of it to indicate the flavour. After all, actors can supply their own accents—Mrs. Quickly, for example, should be rendered in demotic Cockney. Even so some of her malapropisms are reduced or explained for the reader; others may be guessed at, like Shakespeare's bawdy, where he never fails to make a sexual innuendo to tickle the audience.

A favourite word, puissance or puissant, gives difficulty: with Shakespeare it was pronounced as a tri-syllable, pù-issance. I have replaced it: the adjective 'powerful' is conveniently tri-syllabic. Words like hour, tire or tired, prayer, were pronounced as two syllables. The personal 'who' and impersonal 'which' are interchangeable and used quite inconsistently by Shakespeare: I have regularised them to accord with modern usage. Similarly with 'on' and 'of' which are used interchangeably. Shakespeare's ungrammatical use of 'who' for 'whom' points the way the language is moving, with careless writers, today. The use of the subordinate verb to be, 'is come' for 'has come', is oddly in accordance with French usage, and should be regularised—let alone redundant 'that', as in 'if that', 'for that', etc.

It is worth noting that the phrase several times repeated on Pistol's flamboyant lips—he regularly talks inflated nonsense—'And that's the humour of it' is a joke, kindly enough, against the 'Humour' plays which Ben Jonson patented just at this time. Shakespeare welcomed his play, *Every Man in his Humour*, to the Chamberlain's Men in 1598, and himself acted in Ben's *Every Man out of his Humour* next year, the year of *Henry V*. To know these connexions makes the stage-life of the time more real to us.

CHARACTERS

CHORUS

KING HENRY THE FIFTH
DUKE OF GLOUCESTER
DUKE OF BEDFORD   } brothers of the King
DUKE OF CLARENCE
DUKE OF EXETER, uncle of the King
DUKE OF YORK, cousin of the King
EARL OF SALISBURY
EARL OF WESTMORLAND
EARL OF WARWICK
EARL OF HUNTINGDON
ARCHBISHOP OF CANTERBURY
BISHOP OF ELY
RICHARD EARL OF CAMBRIDGE
HENRY LORD SCROOP   } conspirators
SIR THOMAS GREY
SIR THOMAS ERPINGHAM
CAPTAIN FLUELLEN
CAPTAIN GOWER   } officers
CAPTAIN JAMY
CAPTAIN MACMORRIS
JOHN BATES
ALEXANDER COURT   } soldiers
MICHAEL WILLIAMS
BARDOLPH
NYM
PISTOL   } camp-followers
BOY
HOSTESS QUICKLY, now married to Pistol

CHARLES THE SIXTH, King of France

LEWIS, the Dauphin
DUKE OF BURGUNDY
DUKE OF ORLEANS
DUKE OF BRITAINE
DUKE OF BOURBON
CHARLES DELABRETH, Constable of France
GRANDPRÉ ⎫
              ⎬   French Lords
RAMBURES ⎭
THE GOVERNOR OF HARFLEUR
MONTJOY, a French Herald
AMBASSADORS to the King of England
MONSIEUR LE FER, a French soldier
ISABEL, Queen of France
KATHERINE, daughter of the King of France
ALICE, a lady attending on her

LORDS, LADIES, OFFICERS, SOLDIERS, CITIZENS,
MESSENGERS, HERALDS, ATTENDANTS

Prologue

Flourish. Enter Chorus

CHORUS

O for a Muse of fire, that would ascend
The brightest heaven of inventiòn,
A kingdom for a stage, princes to act,
And monarchs to behold the swelling scene!
Then should the warlike Harry, like himself,
Assume the state of Mars, and at his heels,
Leashed in like hounds, should famine, sword, and fire
Crouch for employment. But pardon, gentles all,
The flat unraisèd spirits that have dared
On this unworthy scaffold to bring forth
So great an object. Can this cockpit hold
The vasty fields of France? Or may we cram
Within this wooden O the very casques
That did affright the air at Agincourt?
O, pardon! since a crookèd figure may
Attest in little place a milliòn,
And let us, ciphers to this great account,
On your imaginary forces work.
Suppose within the girdle of these walls
Are now confined two mighty monarchies,
Whose high uprearèd and abutting fronts
The perilous narrow ocean parts asunder.
Piece out our imperfections with your thoughts:
Into a thousand parts divide one man,
And make an imaginary universe.
Think, when we talk of horses, that you see them
Printing their proud hoofs in the receiving earth;
For 'tis your thoughts that now must deck our kings,

Carry them here and there, jumping over times,
Turning the accomplishment of many years
Into an hour-glass: now for which supply,
Admit me Chorus to this history,
Who Prologue-like your humble patience pray,
Gently to hear, kindly to judge, our play.   *Exit*

Act I

SCENE I
Westminster. The palace.

*Enter the Archbishop of Canterbury and the
Bishop of Ely*

CANTERBURY
My lord, I'll tell you. That self bill is urged
Which in the eleventh year of the last King's reign
Was likely, and had indeed against us passed,
But that the contentious and unquiet time
Did push it out of farther questiòn.

ELY
But how, my lord, shall we resist it now?

CANTERBURY
It must be thought on. If it passes against us,
We lose the better half of our possession.
For all the temporal lands which men devout
By testament have given to the Church
Would they strip from us. Being valued thus—
As much as would maintain, to the King's honour,
Full fifteen earls, and fifteen hundred knights,
Six thousand and two hundred good esquires;
And, to relief of lepers and weak age,
Of indigent faint souls past corporal toil,
A hundred almshouses right well supplied;
And, to the coffers of the King beside,
A thousand pounds by the year. Thus runs the bill.

ELY

This would drink deep.

CANTERBURY   It would drink the cup and all.

ELY

But what prevention?

CANTERBURY

The King is full of grace and fair regard.

ELY

And a true lover of the holy Church.

CANTERBURY

The courses of his youth promised it not.
The breath no sooner left his father's body
But that his wildness, mortified in him,
Seemed to die too. Yea, at that very moment,
Consideration like an angel came
And whipped the offending Adam out of him,
Leaving his body as a paradise
To envelop and contain celestial spirits.
Never was such a sudden scholar made;
Never came reformation in a flood
With such a heady current scouring faults.
Nor ever Hydra-headed wilfulness
So soon did lose its seat, and all at once,
As in this King.

ELY   We are blessèd in the change.

CANTERBURY

Hear him but reason in divinity,
And all-admiring, with an inward wish,
You would desire the King were made a prelate.
Hear him debate of commonwealth affairs,
You would say it has been all in all his study.
List his discourse of war, and you shall hear
A fearful battle rendered you in music.
Turn him to any cause of policy,
The Gordian knot of it he will unloose,
Familiar as his garter; that, when he speaks,

The air, a chartered libertine, is still,
And the mute wonder lurks then in men's ears
To steal his sweet and honeyed sentences.
So that the art and practical part of life
Must be the mistress to the theory—
Which is a wonder how his grace should glean it,
Since his addiction was to courses vain,
His companies unlettered, rude, and shallow;
His hours filled up with riots, banquets, sports,
And never noted in him any study,
Any retirement, any sequestration,
From open haunts and popularity.

ELY

The strawberry grows underneath the nettle,
And wholesome berries thrive and ripen best
Neighboured by fruit of baser quality.
And so the Prince obscured his contemplation
Under the veil of wildness—which, no doubt,
Grew like the summer grass, fastest by night,
Unseen, yet growing in capacity.

CANTERBURY

It must be so, for miracles are ceased;
And therefore we must needs admit the means
How things are pèrfected.

ELY   But, my good lord,
How now for mitigation of this bill
Urged by the Commons? Does his majesty
Incline to it, or no?

CANTERBURY   He seems impartial,
Or rather swaying more upon our part
Than cherishing the exhibiters against us.
For I have made an offer to his majesty—
Upon our spiritual Convocation,
And in regard of causes now in hand,
Which I have opened to his grace at large
As touching France—to give a greater sum

Than ever at one time the clergy yet
Did to his predecessors part with free.

ELY

How did this offer seem received, my lord?

CANTERBURY

With good acceptance of his majesty,
Save that there was not time enough to hear—
As I perceived his grace would fain have done—
The several and unhidden passages
Of his true titles to some certain dukedoms,
And generally to the crown and seat of France,
Derived from Edward, his great-grandfather.

ELY

What was the impediment that broke this off?

CANTERBURY

The French ambassador upon that instant
Craved audience, and the hour, I think, is come
To give him hearing. Is it four o'clock?

ELY

It is.

CANTERBURY

Then go we in to know his embassy;
Which I could with a ready guess declare
Before the Frenchman speaks a word of it.

ELY

I'll wait upon you, and I long to hear it.

Exeunt

SCENE II
The same.

*Enter the King, Gloucester, Bedford, Clarence,
Exeter, Warwick, Westmorland, and attendants*

KING HENRY
    Where is my gracious Lord of Canterbury?
EXETER
    Not here in presence.
KING HENRY   Send for him, good uncle.
WESTMORLAND
    Shall we call in the ambassador, my liege?
KING HENRY
    Not yet, my cousin; we would be resolved,
    Before we hear him, of some things of weight
    That tax our thoughts, concerning us and France.

*Enter the Archbishop of Canterbury and the Bishop
of Ely*

CANTERBURY
    God and His angels guard your sacred throne,
    And make you long become it!
KING HENRY   Sure, we thank you.
    My learnèd lord, we pray you to proceed,
    And justly and religiously unfold
    Why the law Salic that they have in France
    Either should or should not bar us in our claim.
    And God forbid, my dear and faithful lord,
    That you should fashion, wrest, or bow your reading,
    Or nicely charge your understanding soul
    With opening titles miscreate, whose right
    Suits not in native colours with the truth.
    For God does know how many now in health
    Shall drop their blood in approbatiòn
    Of what your reverence shall incite us to.
    Therefore take heed how you impawn our person,
    How you awake our sleeping sword of war.
    We charge you in the name of God, take heed;
    For never two such kingdoms did contend
    Without much fall of blood, whose guiltless drops

Are every one a woe, a sore complaint
Against him whose wrongs give edge unto the swords
That make such waste in brief mortality.
Under this conjuration speak, my lord,
For we will hear, note, and believe in heart
That what you speak is in your conscience washed
As pure as sin with baptism.

CANTERBURY

Then hear me, gracious sovereign, and you peers,
That owe yourselves, your lives, and services
To this imperial throne. There is no bar
To make against your highness' claim to France
But this, which they produce from Pharamond:
'In terram Salicam mulieres ne succedant'—
'No woman shall succeed in Salic land'.
Which Salic land the French unjustly gloss
To be the realm of France, and Pharamond
The founder of this law and female bar.
Yet their own authors faithfully affirm
That the land Salic is in Germany,
Between the floods of Sala and of Elbe.
Where Charles the Great, having subdued the Saxons,
There left behind and settled certain French,
Who, holding in disdain the German women
For some dishonest manners of their life,
Established then this law: to wit, no female
Should be inheritrix in Salic land.
Which Salic, as I said, between Elbe and Sala,
Is at this day in Germany called Meisen.
Then does it well appear the Salic law
Was not devisèd for the realm of France.
Nor did the French possess the Salic land
Until four hundred one-and-twenty years
After defunction of King Pharamond,
Idly supposed the founder of this law,
Who died within the year of our redemption

Four hundred twenty-six. And Charles the Great
Subdued the Saxons, and did seat the French
Beyond the river Sala, in the year
Eight hundred five. Besides, their writers say,
King Pepin, who deposèd Childeric,
Did, as heir general, being descended
Of Blithild, who was daughter to King Clothair,
Make claim and title to the crown of France.
Hugh Capet also—who usurped the crown
Of Charles the Duke of Lorraine, sole heir male
Of the true line and stock of Charles the Great—
To find his title with some shows of truth,
Though in pure truth it was corrupt and naught,
Conveyed himself as the heir to the Lady Lingard,
Daughter to Charlemain, who was the son
To Lewis the Emperor, and Lewis the son
Of Charles the Great. Also King Lewis the Ninth,
Who was sole heir to the usurper Capet,
Could not keep quiet in his consciènce,
Wearing the crown of France, till satisfied
That fair Queen Isabel, his grandmother,
Was lineal of the Lady Ermengard,
Daughter to Charles the foresaid Duke of Lorraine.
By which marriage the line of Charles the Great
Was re-united to the crown of France.
So that, as clear as is the summer's sun,
King Pepin's title, and Hugh Capet's claim,
King Lewis's satisfaction, all appear
To hold in right and title of the female.
So do the kings of France unto this day,
Howbeit they would hold up this Salic law
To bar your highness claiming from the female,
And rather choose to hide them in a net
Than amply to unbar their crookèd titles
Usurped from you and your progenitors.

KING HENRY

  May I with right and conscience make this claim?

CANTERBURY

  The sin upon my head, dread sovereign!
  For in the Book of Numbers is it written,
  When the man dies, let the inheritance
  Descend unto the daughter. Gracious lord,
  Stand for your own, unwind your bloody flag,
  Look back into your mighty ancestors.
  Go, my dread lord, to your great-grandsire's tomb,
  From whom you claim; invoke his warlike spirit,
  And your great-uncle's, Edward the Black Prince,
  Who on the French ground played a tragedy,
  Making defeat on the full power of France,
  While his most mighty father on a hill
  Stood smiling to behold his lion's whelp
  Forage in blood of French nobility.
  O noble English, that could entertain
  With half their forces the full pride of France,
  And let another half stand laughing by,
  All out of work and cold for actiòn!

ELY

  Awake remembrance of these valiant dead,
  And with your powerful arm renew their feats.
  You are their heir, you sit upon their throne,
  The blood and courage that renownèd them
  Runs in your veins; and my thrice-mighty liege
  Is in the very May-morn of his youth,
  Ripe for exploits and mighty enterprises.

EXETER

  Your brother kings and monarchs of the earth
  Do all expect that you should rouse yourself,
  As did the former lions of your blood.

WESTMORLAND

  They know your grace has cause and means and might—
  So has your highness. Never King of England

Had nobles richer and more loyal subjects,
Whose hearts have left their bodies here in England
And lie pavilioned in the fields of France.

CANTERBURY

O, let their bodies follow, my dear liege,
With blood and sword and fire to win your right!
In aid whereof we of the spiritualty
Will raise your highness such a mighty sum
As never did the clergy at one time
Bring in to any of your ancestors.

KING HENRY

We must not only arm to invade the French
But lay down our proportions to defend
Against the Scot, who will make road upon us
With all advantages.

CANTERBURY

They of those marches, gracious sovereign,
Shall be a wall sufficient to defend
Our inland from the pilfering borderers.

KING HENRY

We do not mean the coursing snatchers only,
But fear the main intention of the Scot,
Who has been ever a giddy neighbour to us.
For you shall read that my great-grandfather
Never went with his forces into France
But that the Scot on his unfurnished kingdom
Came pouring, like the tide into a breach,
With ample and brim fullness of his force,
Galling the gleanèd land with hot assaults,
Girding with grievous siege castles and towns;
That England, being empty of defence,
Shook and trembled at the ill neighbourhood.

CANTERBURY

She has been then more feared than harmed, my liege;
For hear her but exampled by herself:
When all her chivalry has been in France,

And she a mourning widow of her nobles,
She has herself not only well defended
But taken and impounded as a stray
The King of Scots: whom she did send to France
To fill King Edward's fame with prisoner kings,
And make her chronicle as rich with praise
As is the ooze and bottom of the sea
With sunken wreck and sumless treasuries.

ELY

But there's a saying very old and true:
   'If that you will France win,
    Then with Scotland first begin.'
For once the eagle England being in prey,
To her unguarded nest the weasel Scot
Comes sneaking, and so sucks her princely eggs,
Playing the mouse in absence of the cat,
To wreck and havoc more than she can eat.

EXETER

It follows then the cat must stay at home;
Yet that is but a crushed necessity,
Since we have locks to safeguard necessaries,
And pretty traps to catch the petty thieves.
While the armèd hand does fight abroad,
The advisèd head defends itself at home;
For government, though high, and low, and lower,
Put into parts, does keep in one consent,
Agreeing in a full and natural close,
Like music.

CANTERBURY   True: therefore does heaven divide
The state of man in divers functiòns,
Setting endeavour in continual motion;
To which is fixèd as an aim or butt
Obedience; for so work the honey-bees,
Creatures that by a rule in nature teach
The act of order to a peopled kingdom.
They have a king, and officers of sorts,

Where some, like magistrates, correct at home;
Others, like merchants, venture trade abroad.
Others, like soldiers, armèd in their stings,
Make booty of the summer's velvet buds:
Which pillage they with merry march bring home
To the tent-royal of their emperor.
Who, busied in his majesties, surveys
The singing masons building roofs of gold,
The civil citizens kneading up the honey,
The poor mechanic porters crowding in
Their heavy burdens at his narrow gate,
The sad-eyed justice, with his surly hum,
Delivering to executors pale
The lazy yawning drone. I this infer,
That many things, having full reference
To one consent, may work contrariously,
As many arrows loosèd several ways
Come to one mark;
As many several ways meet in one town,
As many fresh streams meet in one salt sea,
As many lines close in the dial's centre.
So may a thousand actions, once afoot,
End in one purpose, and be all well borne
Without defeat. Therefore to France, my liege!
Divide your happy England into four;
Whereof take you one quarter into France,
And you with that shall make all Gallia shake.
If we, with thrice such powèrs left at home,
Cannot defend our own doors from the dog,
Let us be worried, and our nation lose
The name of hardiness and policy.

KING HENRY

Call in the messengers sent from the Dauphin.

Exeunt some attendants

Now are we well resolved, and by God's help
And yours, the noble sinews of our power,

France being ours, we'll bend it to our awe,
Or break it all to pieces. Or there we'll sit,
Ruling in large and ample empery
Over France and her almost kingly dukedoms,
Or lay these bones in an unworthy urn,
Tombless, with no remembrance over them.
Either our history shall with full mouth
Speak freely of our acts, or else our grave,
Like Turkish mute, shall have a tongueless mouth,
Not worshipped with a waxen epitaph.

Enter Ambassadors of France

Now are we well prepared to know the pleasure
Of our fair cousin Dauphin; for we hear
Your greeting is from him, not from the King.
AMBASSADOR
May it please your majesty to give us leave
Freely to render what we have in charge,
Or shall we sparingly show you far off
The Dauphin's meaning and our embassy?
KING HENRY
We are no tyrant, but a Christian king,
Unto whose grace our passion is as subject
As are our wretches fettered in our prisons:
Therefore with frank and with uncurbèd plainness
Tell us the Dauphin's mind.
AMBASSADOR   Thus then, in short:
Your highness, lately sending into France,
Did claim some certain dukedoms, in the right
Of your great predecessor, King Edward the Third.
In answer of which claim, the Prince our master
Says that you savour too much of your youth,
And bids you be advised there's naught in France
That can be with a nimble galliard won;
You cannot revel into dukedoms there.

He therefore sends you, meeter for your spirit,
This tun of treasure; and, in lieu of this,
Desires you let the dukedoms that you claim
Hear no more of you. This the Dauphin speaks.

KING HENRY
What treasure, uncle?

EXETER   Tennis-balls, my liege.

KING HENRY
We are glad the Dauphin is so pleasant with us.
His present, and your pains, we thank you for.
When we have matched our rackets to these balls,
We will in France, by God's grace, play a set
Shall strike his father's crown into the hazard.
Tell him he has made a match with such a wrangler
That all the courts of France will be disturbed
With chases. And we understand him well,
How he comes over us with our wilder days,
Not measuring what use we made of them.
We never valued this poor seat of England,
And therefore, living hence, did give ourself
To barbarous licence; as it is ever common
That men are merriest when away from home.
But tell the Dauphin I will keep my state,
Be like a king, and show my sail of greatness,
When I do rouse me in my throne of France.
For then I have laid by my majesty,
And plodded like a man for working-days;
But I will rise there with so full a glory
That I will dazzle all the eyes of France,
Yea, strike the Dauphin blind to look on us.
And tell the pleasant Prince this mock of his
Has turned his balls to gun-stones, and his soul
Shall stand sore chargèd for the wasteful vengeance
That shall fly with them. For many a thousand widows
Shall this his mock mock out of their dear husbands;
Mock mothers from their sons, mock castles down;

And some are yet ungotten and unborn
That shall have cause to curse the Dauphin's scorn.
But this lies all within the will of God,
To whom I do appeal, and in whose name,
Tell you the Dauphin, I am coming on,
To revenge me as I may, and to put forth
My rightful hand in a well-hallowed cause.
So get you hence in peace; and tell the Dauphin
His jest will savour but of shallow wit
When thousands weep more than did laugh at it.
Convey them with safe conduct. Fare you well.

Exeunt Ambassadors

EXETER

This was a merry message.

KING HENRY

We hope to make the sender blush at it.
Therefore, my lords, omit no happy hour
That may give furtherance to our expedition;
For we have now no thought in us but France,
Save those to God, that run before our business.
Therefore let our proportions for these wars
Be soon collected, and all things thought upon
That may with reasonable swiftness add
More feathers to our wings; for, God before,
We'll chide this Dauphin at his father's door.
Therefore let every man now task his thought
That this fair action may on foot be brought. *Exeunt*

Prologue to Act II

Flourish. Enter Chorus

CHORUS

Now all the youth of England are on fire,
And silken dalliance in the wardrobe lies.
Now thrive the armourers, and honour's thought
Reigns solely in the breast of every man.
They sell the pasture now to buy the horse,
Following the mirror of all Christian kings
With wingèd heels, as English Mercuries.
For now sits expectation in the air,
And hides a sword from hilt unto the point
With crowns imperial, crowns and coronets,
Promised to Harry and his followers.
The French, advised by good intelligence
Of this most dreadful preparatiòn,
Shake in their fear, and with pale policy
Seek to divert the English purposes.
O England! model to your inward greatness,
Like little body with a mighty heart,
What might you do, that honour would you do,
Were all your children kind and natural!
But see, your fault France has in you found out,
A nest of hollow bosoms, which he fills
With treacherous crowns. And three corrupted men—
One, Richard Earl of Cambridge, and the second,
Henry Lord Scroop of Masham, and the third,
Sir Thomas Grey, knight, of Northumberland—
Have, for the gilt of France—O guilt indeed!—
Confirmed conspiracy with fearful France.
And by their hands this grace of kings must die,

39

If hell and treason hold their promises,
Ere he takes ship for France, and in Southampton.
Linger your patience on, and we'll digest
The abuse of distance, forge a play.
The sum is paid; the traitors are agreed;
The King is set from London; and the scene
Is now transported, gentles, to Southampton.
There is the playhouse now, there must you sit,
And thence to France shall we convey you safe
And bring you back, charming the narrow seas
To give you gentle pass; for, if we may,
We'll not offend one stomach with our play.
But till the King comes forth, and not till then,
Unto Southampton do we shift our scene.   *Exit*

Act II

SCENE I
London. A street.

Enter Corporal Nym and Lieutenant Bardolph

BARDOLPH   Well met, Corporal Nym.

NYM   Good morrow, Lieutenant Bardolph.

BARDOLPH   What, are Ancient[1] Pistol and you friends yet?

NYM   For my part, I care not. I say little; but when time shall serve, there shall be smiles—but that shall be as it may. I dare not fight, but I will wink and hold out my iron. It is a simple one, but what though? It will toast cheese, and it will endure cold as another man's sword will—and there's an end.

BARDOLPH   I will bestow a breakfast to make you friends, and we'll be all three sworn brothers to France. Let it be so, good Corporal Nym.

NYM   Faith, I will live so long as I may, that's the certain of it; and when I cannot live any longer, I will do as I may. That is my rest, that is the rendezvous of it.

BARDOLPH   It is certain, Corporal, that he is married to Nell Quickly, and certainly she did you wrong, for you were betrothed to her.

NYM   I cannot tell; things must be as they may. Men may sleep, and they may have their throats about them at that time, and some say knives have edges: it must be as it may—though patience is a tired mare, yet she will plod; there must be conclusions—well, I cannot tell.

---

[1]Ensign.

Enter Pistol and Hostess Quickly

BARDOLPH   Here comes Ancient Pistol and his wife. Good
    Corporal, be patient here.
NYM   How now, my host Pistol?
PISTOL
    Base tike, call you me host?
    Now by this hand I swear I scorn the term;
    Nor shall my Nell keep lodgers.
HOSTESS   No, by my word, not long; for we cannot lodge
    and board a dozen or fourteen gentlewomen that live
    honestly by the prick of their needles but it will be
    thought we keep a bawdy-house straight.

Nym draws his sword

    O well-a-day, Lady, if he is not drawn now! We shall see
    wilful adultery and murder committed.
BARDOLPH   Good Lieutenant! Good Corporal! Offer
    nothing here.
NYM   Pish!
PISTOL
    Pish for you, Iceland dog! you prick-eared cur of Iceland!
HOSTESS   Good Corporal Nym, show your valour, and
    put up your sword.
NYM   Will you shog off? I would have you *solus*. [alone].

He sheathes his sword

PISTOL
    '*Solus*', egregious dog? O viper vile!
    The '*solus*' in your most marvellous face!
    The '*solus*' in your teeth and in your throat,
    And in your hateful lungs, yea, in your maw, by God!
    And, which is worse, within your nasty mouth!

I do retort the '*solus*' in your bowels,
For I can take, and Pistol's cock is up,
And flashing fire will follow.

NYM   I am not Barbason; you cannot conjure me. I have
an humour to knock you indifferently well. If you grow
foul with me, Pistol, I will scour you with my rapier, as
I may, in fair terms. If you would walk off, I would prick
your guts a little, in good terms, as I may, and that's the
humour of it.

PISTOL

O braggart vile, and damnèd furious wight!
The grave does gape, and doting death is near:
Therefore exhale!

They both draw

BARDOLPH   Hear me, hear me what I say! He that strikes
the first stroke, I'll run him up to the hilt, as I am a
soldier.

He draws

PISTOL

An oath of much might, and fury shall abate.

Pistol and Nym sheathe their swords

Give me your fist, your forefoot to me give;
Your spirits are most tall.

NYM   I will cut your throat one time or other, in fair
terms, that is the humour of it.

PISTOL

'*Couple a gorge!*'[2]
That is the word. I you defy again!

---

[2]Cut a throat.

O hound of Crete, think you my spouse to get?
No, to the hospital go,
And from the powdering tub of infamy
Fetch forth the leper kite of Cressid's kind,
Doll Tearsheet she by name, and her espouse.
I have, and I will hold, the quondam[3] Quickly
For the only she; and—*pauca,*[4] there's enough.
Go to!

Enter the Boy

BOY   My host Pistol, you must come to my master—and
you, Hostess: he is very sick, and would to bed. Good
Bardolph, put your face between his sheets, and do the
office of a warming-pan. Faith, he's very ill.

BARDOLPH   Away, you rogue!

HOSTESS   By my word, he'll yield the crow a pudding one
of these days; the King has killed his heart. Good
husband, come home presently.   *Exit with Boy*

BARDOLPH   Come, shall I make you two friends? We
must to France together: why the devil should we keep
knives to cut one another's throats?

PISTOL

Let floods o'erswell, and fiends for food howl on!

NYM   You'll pay me the eight shillings I won of you at
betting?

PISTOL

Base is the slave that pays!

NYM   That now I will have; that's the humour of it.

PISTOL

As manhood shall compound. Push home!

They draw

---

[3]Former.
[4]Briefly.

BARDOLPH   By this sword, he that makes the first thrust,
I'll kill him! By this sword, I will.

PISTOL

Sword is an oath, and oaths must have their course.

He sheathes his sword

BARDOLPH   Corporal Nym, if you will be friends, be
friends: if you will not, why then be enemies with me
too. Pray put up.

NYM   I shall have my eight shillings I won of you at
betting?

PISTOL

A crown shall you have, and present pay;
And liquor likewise will I give to you,
And friendship shall combine, and brotherhood.
I'll live by Nym, and Nym shall live by me.
Is not this just? For I shall sutler be
Unto the camp, and profits will accrue.
Give me your hand.

Nym sheathes his sword

NYM   I shall have my crown?

PISTOL

In cash most justly paid.

NYM   Well then, that's the humour of it.

Enter Hostess

HOSTESS   As ever you came of women, come in quickly
to Sir John. Ah, poor heart! he is so shaked of a burning
quotidian fever that it is most lamentable to behold.
Sweet men, come to him.

NYM   The King has run bad humours on the knight,
   that's the truth of it.
PISTOL
   Nym, you have spoken the right;
   His heart is fracted and corroborate.
NYM   The King is a good king, but it must be as it may:
   he passes some humours and careers.
PISTOL
   Let us condole the knight; for, lambkins, we will live.

                                              Exeunt

SCENE II
Southampton. A chamber.

Enter Exeter, Bedford, and Westmorland

BEDFORD
   Before God, his grace is bold to trust these traitors.
EXETER
   They shall be apprehended by and by.
WESTMORLAND
   How smooth and even they do bear themselves!
   As if allegiance in their bosoms sat,
   Crownèd with faith and constant loyalty.
BEDFORD
   The King has note of all that they intend,
   By interception which they dream not of.
EXETER
   Nay, but the man that was his bedfellow,
   Whom he has dulled and cloyed with gracious favours—
   That he should, for a foreign purse, so sell
   His sovereign's life to death and treachery!

*Sound trumpets. Enter the King, Scroop, Cambridge,
             Grey, and attendants*

KING HENRY

Now sits the wind fair, and we will aboard.
My Lord of Cambridge, and my kind Lord of Masham,
And you, my gentle knight, give me your thoughts.
Think you not that the powers we bear with us
Will cut their passage through the force of France,
Doing the execution and the act
For which we have in head assembled them?

SCROOP

No doubt, my liege, if each man does his best.

KING HENRY

I doubt not that, since we are well persuaded
We carry not a heart with us from hence
That grows not in a fair consent with ours;
Nor leave any behind that does not wish
Success and conquest to attend on us.

CAMBRIDGE

Never was monarch better feared and loved
Than is your majesty. There's not, I think, a subject
That sits in heart-grief and uneasiness
Under the sweet shade of your government.

GREY

True: those that were your father's enemies
Have steeped their galls in honey, and do serve you
With hearts created of duty and of zeal.

KING HENRY

We therefore have great cause of thankfulness,
And shall forget the office of our hand
Sooner than quittance of desert and merit
According to the weight and worthiness.

SCROOP

So service shall with steelèd sinews toil,
And labour shall refresh itself with hope
To do your grace incessant services.

KING HENRY

    We judge no less. Uncle of Exeter,

    Enlarge the man committed yesterday

    That railed against our person. We consider

    It was excess of wine that set him on,

    And on his more advice we pardon him.

SCROOP

    That's mercy, but too much security.

    Let him be punished, sovereign, lest example

    Breed, by his sufferance, more of such a kind.

KING HENRY

    O, let us yet be merciful.

CAMBRIDGE

    So may your highness, and yet punish too.

GREY

    Sir,

    You show great mercy if you give him life

    After the taste of much correctiòn.

KING HENRY

    Alas, your too much love and care of me

    Are heavy orisons against this poor wretch!

    If little faults, proceeding on distemper,

    Shall not be winked at, how shall we stretch our eye

    When capital crimes, chewed, swallowed, and digested,

    Appear before us? We'll yet enlarge that man,

    Though Cambridge, Scroop, and Grey, in their dear
       care

    And tender preservation of our person

    Would have him punished. And now to our French
       causes:

    Who are the late commissioners?

CAMBRIDGE

    I one, my lord.

    Your highness bade me ask for it today.

SCROOP
  So did you me, my liege.

GREY
  And I, my royal sovereign.

KING HENRY
  Then, Richard Earl of Cambridge, there is yours;
  There yours, Lord Scroop of Masham; and, sir knight,
  Grey of Northumberland, this same is yours.
  Read them, and know I know your worthiness.
  My Lord of Westmorland, and uncle Exeter,
  We will aboard tonight.—Why, how now, gentlemen?
  What see you in those papers, that you lose
  So much complexion? Look you, how they change!
  Their cheeks are paper.—Why, what read you there
  That have so cowarded and chased your blood
  Out of appearance?

CAMBRIDGE   I do confess my fault,
  And do submit me to your highness' mercy.

GREY, SCROOP
  To which we all appeal.

KING HENRY
  The mercy that was quick in us but late
  By your own counsel is suppressed and killed.
  You must not dare, for shame, to talk of mercy,
  For your own reasons turn into your bosoms
  As dogs upon their masters, worrying you.
  See you, my princes, and my noble peers,
  These English monsters! My Lord of Cambridge here—
  You know how apt our love was to accord
  To furnish him with all appertinents
  Belonging to his honour. And this man
  Has, for a few light crowns, lightly conspired,
  And sworn unto the practices of France,
  To kill us here in Hampton. To which also
  This knight, no less for bounty bound to us
  Than Cambridge is, has likewise sworn. But O,

What shall I say to you, Lord Scroop, you cruel,
Ungrateful, savage, and inhuman creature?
You that did bear the key of all my counsels,
That knew the very bottom of my soul,
That almost might have coined me into gold,
Would you have practised on me, for your use?
May it be possible that foreign hire
Could out of you extract one spark of evil
That might annoy my finger? It is so strange
That, though the truth of it stands off as gross
As black and white, my eye will scarcely see it.
Treason and murder ever kept together,
As two yoke-devils sworn to either's purpose,
Working so grossly in a natural cause
That astonishment did not whoop at them.
But you, against all proportion, did bring in
Wonder to wait on treason and on murder:
And whatsoever cunning fiend it was
That wrought upon you so preposterously
Has got the voice in hell for excellence.
All other devils that suggest by treasons
Do botch and bungle up damnatìon
With patches, colours, and with forms, being fetched
From glistering semblances of piety.
But he that tempered you bade you stand up,
Gave you no instance why you should do treason,
Unless to dub you with the name of traitor.
If that same demon that has gulled you thus
Should with his lion gait walk the whole world,
He might return to vast Tartary back,
And tell the legions, 'I can never win
A soul so easy as that Englishman's.'
O, how have you with deep mistrust infected
The sweetness of affiance! Show men dutiful?
Why, so did you. Seem they grave and learnèd?
Why, so did you. Come they of noble family?

Why, so did you. Seem they religious?
Why, so did you. Or are they spare in diet,
Free from gross passion or of mirth or anger,
Constant in spirit, not swerving with the blood,
Garnished and decked in modest complement,
Not working with the eye without the ear,
And but in purgèd judgement trusting neither?
Such and so finely sifted did you seem:
And thus your fall has left a kind of blot
To mark the thoughtful man and best endued
With some suspicion. I will weep for you;
For this revolt of yours, I think, is like
Another fall of man. Their faults are open.
Arrest them to the answer of the law;
And God acquit them of their practices!

EXETER   I arrest you of high treason, by the name of
Richard Earl of Cambridge.
I arrest you of high treason, by the name of Henry Lord
Scroop of Masham.
I arrest you of high treason, by the name of Thomas
Grey, knight, of Northumberland.

SCROOP

Our purposes God justly has discovered,
And I repent my fault more than my death.
Which I beseech your highness to forgive,
Although my body pays the price of it.

CAMBRIDGE

For me, the gold of France did not seduce,
Although I did admit it as a motive
The sooner to effect what I intended.
But God be thankèd for prevention,
Which I in sufferance heartily will rejoice,
Beseeching God and you to pardon me.

GREY

Never did faithful subject more rejoice
At the discovery of most dangerous treason

Than I do at this hour joy o'er myself,
Prevented from a damnèd enterprise.
My fault, but not my body, pardon, sovereign.
KING HENRY
God quit you in His mercy! Hear your sentence.
You have conspired against our royal person,
Joined with an enemy proclaimed, and from his coffers
Received the golden earnest of our death.
Wherein you would have sold your King to slaughter,
His princes and his peers to servitude,
His subjects to oppression and contempt,
And his whole kingdom into desolation.
Touching our person seek we no revenge,
But we our kingdom's safety must so tender,
Whose ruin you have sought, that to her laws
We do deliver you. Get you therefore hence,
Poor miserable wretches, to your death;
The taste whereof God of His mercy give
You patience to endure, and true repentance
Of all your dire offences. Bear them hence.

Exeunt Cambridge, Scroop, and Grey, guarded

Now, lords, for France; the enterprise whereof
Shall be to you, as us, like glorious.
We doubt not of a fair and lucky war,
Since God so graciously has brought to light
This dangerous treason lurking in our way
To hinder our beginnings. We doubt not now
But every rub is smoothèd on our way.
Then forth, dear countrymen! Let us deliver
Our armament into the hand of God,
Putting it straight in expeditìon.
Cheerily to sea! The signs of war advance!
No King of England if not King of France!
                                    Flourish. Exeunt

SCENE III
London. Before the Boar's Head.

Enter Pistol, Hostess, Nym, Bardolph, and Boy

HOSTESS   Pray, honey-sweet husband, let me bring you to
Staines.

PISTOL

No, for my manly heart does grieve.
Bardolph, be blithe! Nym, rouse your vaunting veins!
Boy, bristle your courage up! For Falstaff, he is dead,
And we must grieve therefor.

BARDOLPH   Would I were with him, wheresoever he is,
either in heaven or in hell!

HOSTESS   Nay, sure, he's not in hell: he's in Arthur's
bosom, if ever man went to Arthur's bosom. He made a
finer end, and went away as it had been any christened
child; he departed even just between twelve and one,
even at the turning of the tide. For after I saw him
fumble with the sheets, and play with flowers, and
smile upon his fingers' ends, I knew there was but one
way; for his nose was as sharp as a pen, and he talked of
green fields. 'How now, Sir John?' said I, 'What, man, be
of good cheer!' So he cried out, 'God, God, God!' three or
four times. Now I, to comfort him, bid him he should
not think of God—I hoped there was no need to trouble
himself with any such thoughts yet. So he bade me lay
more clothes on his feet; I put my hand into the bed,
and felt them, and they were as cold as any stone; then I
felt to his knees, and so upward and upward, and all
was as cold as any stone.

NYM   They say he cried out for sack.

HOSTESS   Ay, that he did.

BARDOLPH   And for women.

HOSTESS   Nay, that he did not.

BOY   Yes, that he did, and said they were devils incarnate.

HOSTESS   He could never abide carnation, 'twas a colour he never liked.

BOY   He said once, the devil would have him about women.

HOSTESS   He did in some sort, indeed, handle women; but then he was rheumatic, and talked of the Whore of Babylon.

BOY   Do you not remember, he saw a flea stick upon Bardolph's nose, and he said it was a black soul burning in hell?

BARDOLPH   Well, the fuel is gone that maintained that fire—that's all the riches I got in his service.

NYM   Shall we be off? The King will be gone from Southampton.

PISTOL

Come, let's away. My love, give me your lips.

Look to my chattels and my movables.

Let senses rule. The word is 'Pitch and pay!'

Trust none;

For oaths are straws, men's faiths are wafer-cakes,

And Holdfast is the only dog, my duck.

Therefore, *Caveto* [Take care] be your counsellor.

Go, clear your crystals. Yoke-fellows in arms,

Let us to France, like horse-leeches, my boys,

To suck, to suck, the very blood to suck!

BOY   And that's but unwholesome food, they say.

PISTOL

Touch her soft mouth, and march.

BARDOLPH   Farewell, Hostess.

He kisses her

NYM   I cannot kiss, that is the humour of it; but adieu.

PISTOL
    Let housewifery appear. Keep close, I you command.
HOSTESS   Farewell! Adieu!   *Exeunt*

SCENE IV
France. The King's palace.

*Flourish. Enter the French King, the Dauphin, the Dukes
of Berri and Brittany, the Constable and others*

FRENCH KING
    Thus come the English with full power upon us,
    And more than carefully it us concerns
    To answer royally in our defences.
    Therefore the Dukes of Berri and of Brittany,
    Of Brabant and of Orleans, shall make forth,
    And you, Prince Dauphin, with all swift dispatch,
    To line and new repair our towns of war
    With men of courage and with means defendant;
    For England's near approaches make as fierce
    As waters to the sucking of a gulf.
    It fits us then to be as provident
    As fear may teach us, out of late examples
    Left by the fatal and neglected English
    Upon our fields.
DAUPHIN   My most redoubted father,
    It is most meet we arm us against the foe;
    For peace itself should not so dull a kingdom,
    Though war nor any quarrel were in question,
    But that defences, musters, preparations,
    Should be maintained, assembled, and collected,
    As if a war's in expectatiòn.
    Therefore, I say, 'tis meet we all go forth
    To view the sick and feeble parts of France:
    And let us do it with no show of fear—

No, with no more than if we heard that England
Were busied with a Whitsun morris-dance.
For, my good liege, she is so idly kinged,
Her sceptre so fantastically borne
By a vain, giddy, shallow, changeable youth,
That fear attends her not.

CONSTABLE   O, peace, Prince Dauphin!
You are too much mistaken in this King.
Question your grace the late ambassadors,
With what great state he heard their embassy,
How well supplied with noble counsellors,
How modest in objection, and with that
How terrible in constant resolution.
And you shall find his vanities foregone
Were but the outside of the Roman Brutus,
Covering discretion with a coat of folly;
As gardeners do with ordure hide those roots
That shall first spring and be most delicate.

DAUPHIN
Well, it is not so, my Lord High Constable;
But though we think it so, it is no matter.
In cases of defence, it is best to weigh
The enemy more mighty than he seems.
So the proportions of defence are filled;
Which of a weak and niggardly projection
Do like a miser spoil his coat with scanting
A little cloth.

FRENCH KING   Think we King Harry strong;
And, princes, look you strongly arm to meet him.
The kindred of him has been fleshed upon us,
And he is bred out of that bloody strain
That haunted us in our familiar paths.
Witness our too much memorable shame
When Crécy battle fatally was struck,
And all our princes captived by the hand
Of that black name, Edward, Black Prince of Wales.

While his mountain sire, on mountain standing,
Up in the air, crowned with the golden sun,
Saw his heroical seed, and smiled to see him,
Mangle the work of nature, and deface
The patterns that by God and by French fathers
Had twenty years been made. This is a stem
Of that victorious stock; and let us fear
The native mightiness and fate of him.

Enter a Messenger

MESSENGER
Ambassadors from Harry King of England
Do crave admittance to your majesty.
FRENCH KING
We'll give them present audience. Go and bring them.
Exeunt Messenger and certain lords
You see this chase is hotly followed, friends.
DAUPHIN
Turn head, and stop pursuit, for coward dogs
Most spend their mouths when what they seem to
threaten
Runs far before them. Good my sovereign,
Take up the English short, and let them know
Of what a monarchy you are the head.
Self-love, my liege, is not so vile a sin
As self-neglecting.

Enter lords, with Exeter and attendants

FRENCH KING   From our brother of England?
EXETER
From him; and thus he greets your majesty:
He wills you, in the name of God Almighty,
That you divest yourself, and lay apart
The borrowed glories that by gift of heaven,

By law of nature and of nations, belong
To him and to his heirs. Namely, the crown,
And all wide-stretchèd honours that pertain
By custom and the ordinance of times
Unto the crown of France. That you may know
It is no sinister nor awkward claim
Picked from the worm-holes of long-vanished days,
Nor from the dust of old oblivion raked,
He sends you this most memorable line,
In every branch truly demonstrative,
Willing you overlook this pedigree.
And when you find him evenly derived
From his most famed of famous ancestors,
Edward the Third, he bids you then resign
Your crown and kingdom, indirectly held
From him, the native and true challenger.

FRENCH KING

Or else what follows?

EXETER

Bloody constraint; for if you hide the crown
Even in your hearts, there will he rake for it.
Therefore in fierce tempest is he coming,
In thunder and in earthquake, like a Jove,
That, if requiring fail, he will compel.
And bids you, in the bowels of the Lord,
Deliver up the crown, and to take mercy
On the poor souls for whom this hungry war
Opens his vasty jaws; and on your head
Turning the widows' tears, the orphans' cries,
The dead men's blood, deprivèd maidens' groans,
For husbands, fathers, and betrothèd lovers
That shall be swallowed in this controversy.
This is his claim, his threatening, and my message—
Unless the Dauphin is in presence here,
To whom expressly I bring greeting too.

FRENCH KING

    For us, we will consider of this further.
    Tomorrow shall you bear our full intent
    Back to our brother of England.

DAUPHIN   For the Dauphin,

    I stand here for him. What to him from England?

EXETER

    Scorn and defiance, slight regard, contempt,
    And anything that may not misbecome
    The mighty sender, does he prize you at.
    Thus says my King: that if your father's highness
    Does not, in grant of all demands at large,
    Sweeten the bitter mock you sent his majesty,
    He'll call you to so hot an answer of it
    That caves and womby vaultages of France
    Shall chide your trespass, and return your mock
    In second accent of his ordinance.

DAUPHIN

    Say, if my father renders fair return,
    It is against my will, for I desire
    Nothing but odds with England. To that end,
    As matching to his youth and vanity,
    I did present him with the Paris balls.

EXETER

    He'll make your Paris Louvre shake for it,
    Were it the mistress Court of mighty Europe:
    And, be assured, you'll find a difference,
    As we his subjects have in wonder found,
    Between the promise of his greener days
    And these he masters now. Now he weighs time
    Even to the utmost grain; that you shall read
    In your own losses, if he stays in France.

FRENCH KING

    Tomorrow shall you know our mind at full.

Flourish

EXETER
> Dispatch us with all speed, lest our King
> Comes here himself to question our delay,
> For he is footed in this land already.

FRENCH KING
> You shall be soon dispatched with fair conditions.
> A night is but small breath and little pause
> To answer matters of this consequence.   *Exeunt*

Prologue to Act III

Flourish. Enter Chorus

CHORUS
Thus with imagined wing our swift scene flies
In motion of no less celerity
Than that of thought. Suppose that you have seen
The well-appointed King at Hampton pier
Embark his royalty, and his brave fleet
With silken streamers the young Phoebus fanning.
Play with your fancies, and in them behold
Upon the hempen tackle ship-boys climbing;
Hear the shrill whistle which does order give
To sounds confused; behold the threaden sails,
Borne with the invisible and creeping wind,
Draw the huge bottoms through the furrowed sea,
Breasting the lofty surge. O, do but think
You stand upon the shore and can behold
A city on the inconstant billows dancing;
For so appears this fleet majestical,
Holding due course to Harfleur. Follow, follow!
Grapple your minds to sternage of this navy,
And leave your England, as dead midnight still,
Guarded with grandsires, babies, and old women,
Either past or not arrived to pith and power.
For who is he whose chin is but enriched
With one appearing hair that will not follow
These culled and choice-drawn cavaliers to France?
Work, work your thoughts, and therein see a siege:
Behold the ordnance on their carriages,
With fatal mouths gaping on girded Harfleur.
Suppose the ambassador from the French comes back;

Tells Harry that the King does offer him
Katherine his daughter and, with her to dowry,
Some petty and unprofitable dukedoms.
The offer likes not; and the nimble gunner
With linstock now the devilish cannon touches,

Alarum, and chambers go off

And down goes all before them. Still be kind,
And eke out our performance with your mind.   *Exit*

Act III

SCENE I
France. Before Harfleur.

Alarum. Enter the King, Exeter, Bedford, Gloucester, other
lords, and soldiers with scaling-ladders

KING HENRY
  Once more unto the breach, dear friends, once more,
  Or close the wall up with our English dead!
  In peace there's nothing so becomes a man
  As modest stillness and humility.
  But when the blast of war blows in our ears,
  Then imitate the action of the tiger;
  Stiffen the sinews, conjure up the blood,
  Disguise fair nature with hard-featured rage.
  Then lend the eye a terrible aspèct;
  Let it pry through the portage of the head
  Like the brass cannon; let the brow o'erwhelm it
  As fearfully as does a gallèd rock
  O'erhang and thrusts out its confounded base,
  Swilled with the wild and wasteful oceàn.
  Now set the teeth, and stretch the nostril wide,
  Hold hard the breath, and bend up every spirit
  To its full height! On, on, you noblest English,
  Whose blood is fetched from fathers of war-proof!—
  Fathers that, like so many Alexanders,
  Have in these parts from morn till even fought,
  And sheathed their swords for lack of argument.
  Dishonour not your mothers; now attest
  That those whom you called fathers did beget you!

Be copy now to men of grosser blood,
And teach them how to war. And you, good yeomen,
Whose limbs were made in England, show us here
The mettle of your pasture; let us swear
That you are worth your breeding—which I doubt not;
For there is none of you so mean and base
That has not noble lustre in your eyes.
I see you stand like greyhounds in the slips,
Straining upon the start. The game's afoot!
Follow your spirit, and upon this charge
Cry, 'God for Harry, England, and Saint George!'
                    Exeunt. Alarum, and chambers go off

SCENE II
The same.

Enter Nym, Bardolph, Pistol, and Boy

BARDOLPH   On, on, on, on, on! To the breach, to the
    breach!

NYM   Pray, Corporal, stay—the knocks are too hot, and,
    for my own part, I have not a case of lives. The humour
    of it is too hot, that is the very plainsong of it.

PISTOL
    The plainsong is most just; for humours do abound.
    Knocks go and come; God's vassals drop and die;
                    And sword and shield,
                        In bloody field,
                    Do win immortal fame.

BOY   Would I were in an alehouse in London! I would
    give all my fame for a pot of ale, and safety.

PISTOL   And I:
                    If wishes would prevail with me,
                    My purpose should not fail with me,
                        But thither would I hie.

BOY   As duly,
                 But not as truly,
                 As bird does sing on bough.

Enter Fluellen

FLUELLEN   Up to the breach, you dogs! Forward, you
    rascals!

He drives them forward

PISTOL
    Be merciful, great Duke, to men of mould!
    Abate your rage, abate your manly rage,
    Abate your rage, great Duke!
    Good fellow bate your rage! Use lenity, sweet chuck!
NYM   These are good humours! Your honour wins bad
    humours.   *Exeunt all but the Boy*
BOY   As young as I am, I have observed these three
    swashbucklers. I am boy to them all three, but all they
    three, though they would serve me, could not be man to
    me; for indeed three such buffoons do not amount to a
    man. For Bardolph, he is white-livered and red-faced;
    by means whereof he faces it out, but fights not. For
    Pistol, he has a killing tongue, and a quiet sword;
    by means whereof he breaks words, and keeps whole
    weapons. For Nym, he has heard that men of few words
    are the best men; and therefore he scorns to say his
    prayers, lest he should be thought a coward. But his few
    bad words are matched with as few good deeds; for he
    never broke any man's head but his own, and that was
    against a post, when he was drunk. They will steal
    anything, and call it purchase. Bardolph stole a lutecase,
    bore it twelve leagues, and sold it for three halfpence.
    Nym and Bardolph are sworn brothers in filching, and
    in Calais they stole a fire-shovel—I knew by that piece

of service the men would carry coals. They would have
me as familiar with men's pockets as their gloves or
their handkerchiefs. Which makes much against my
manhood, if I should take from another's pocket to put
into mine; for it is plain pocketing up of wrongs. I must
leave them, and seek some better service. Their villainy
goes against my weak stomach, and therefore I must
cast it up.   *Exit*

Enter Fluellen, Gower following

GOWER   Captain Fluellen, you must come presently to
the mines. The Duke of Gloucester would speak with
you.

FLUELLEN   To the mines? Tell you the Duke, it is not so
good to come to the mines, for, look you, the mines are
not according to the discipline of the war. The concavities
of it are not sufficient; for, look you, the adversary, you
may discuss unto the Duke, look you, has dug himself
four yard under the countermines. By Jesu, I think he
will plow up all, if there is not better direction.

GOWER   The Duke of Gloucester, to whom the order of
the siege is given, is altogether directed by an Irishman,
a very valiant gentleman, in faith.

FLUELLEN   It is Captain Macmorris, is it not?

GOWER   I think it is.

FLUELLEN   By Jesu, he is an ass, as in the world; I will
verify as much in his beard. He has no more direction
in the true discipline of the wars, look you, of the
Roman discipline, than has a puppy-dog.

Enter Captain Macmorris and Captain Jamy

GOWER   Here he comes, and the Scots captain, Captain
Jamy, with him.

FLUELLEN   Captain Jamy is a marvellous valorous

gentleman, that is certain, and of great expedition and knowledge in the ancient wars, upon my particular knowledge of his direction. By Jesu, he will maintain his argument as well as any military man in the world, in the discipline of the pristine wars of the Romans.

JAMY   I say good-day, Captain Fluellen.

FLUELLEN   Good-even to your worship, good Captain James.

GOWER   How now, Captain Macmorris, have you quit the mines? Have the pioneers given over?

MACMORRIS   By Chrish, la, 'tish ill done! The work ish given over, the trompet sounds the retreat. By my hand I swear, and my father's soul, the work ish ill done: it ish given over. I would have blowed up the town, so Chrish save me, la, in an hour. O, 'tish ill done, 'tish ill done—by my hand, 'tish ill done!

FLUELLEN   Captain Macmorris, I beseech you now, will you give me, look you, a few disputations with you, as partly touching or concerning the discipline of the war, the Roman wars, in the way of argument, look you, and friendly communication?—partly to satisfy my opinion, and partly for the satisfaction, look you, of my mind—as touching the direction of the military discipline, that is the point.

JAMY   It sall be vary gud, gud feith, gud captens bath, and I sall quit you with gud leve, as I may pick occasion: that sall I, for sure.

MACMORRIS   It is no time to discourse, so Chrish save me! The day is hot, and the weather, and the wars, and the King, and the Dukes—it is no time to discourse, the town is besieged, and the trumpet calls us to the breach, and we talk and, be Chrish, do nothing. 'Tis shame for us all: so God save me 'tis shame to stand still, it is shame, by my hand—and there are throats to be cut, and works to be done, and there ish nothing done, so Chrish save me, la!

JAMY   By the mess, ere theise eyes of mine take themselves
  to slomber, ay'll de gud service, or ay'll lie i'th'grund for
  it, ay, or go to death! And ay'll pay't as valorously as I
  may, that sall I suerly do, that is the breff and the long.
  Sure, I wad full fain hear some question 'tween you
  tway.

FLUELLEN   Captain Macmorris, I think, look you, under
  your correction, there is not many of your nation—

MACMORRIS   Of my nation? What ish my nation? Ish a
  villain, and a bastard, and a knave, and a rascal. What
  ish my nation? Who talks of my nation?

FLUELLEN   Look you, if you take the matter otherwise
  than is meant, Captain Macmorris, peradventure I shall
  think you do not use me with that affability as in
  discretion you ought to use me, look you, being as good
  a man as yourself, both in the discipline of war, and in
  the derivation of my birth, and in other particularities.

MACMORRIS   I do not know you so good a man as myself.
  So Chrish save me, I will cut off your head.

GOWER   Gentlemen both, you will mistake each other.

JAMY   Ah, that's a foul fault!

A parley is sounded

GOWER   The town sounds a parley.

FLUELLEN   Captain Macmorris, when there is better
  opportunity to be required, look you, I will be so bold as
  to tell you, I know the discipline of war; and there is an
  end.   *Exeunt*

SCENE III
The same.

*Some citizens of Harfleur appear on the walls. Enter the
King and all his train before the gates*

KING HENRY
    How yet resolves the Governor of the town?
    This is the latest parley we will admit:
    Therefore to our best mercy give yourselves,
    Or, like to men proud of destructiòn,
    Defy us to our worst. For, as I am a soldier,
    A name that in my thoughts becomes me best,
    If I begin the battery once again,
    I will not leave the half-achievèd Harfleur
    Till in her ashes she lie burièd.
    The gates of mercy shall be all shut up,
    And the fleshed soldier, rough and hard of heart,
    In liberty of bloody hand shall range
    With conscience wide as hell, mowing like grass
    Your fresh fair virgins, and your flowering infants.
    What is it then to me, if impious war,
    Arrayed in flames, like to the prince of fiends,
    Does, with his smirched complexion, all fierce feats
    Enlinked to waste and desolatiòn?
    What is it to me, when you yourselves are cause,
    If your pure maidens fall into the hand
    Of hot and forcing violatiòn?
    What rein can hold licentious wickedness
    When down the hill it holds its fierce career?
    We may as fruitless spend our vain command
    Upon the enragèd soldiers in their spoil
    As send precepts to the leviathan
    To come ashore. Therefore, you men of Harfleur,
    Take pity of your town and of your people
    While yet my soldiers are in my command—
    While yet the cool and temperate wind of grace
    O'erblows the filthy and contagious clouds
    Of heady murder, spoil, and villainy.
    If not, why, in a moment look to see
    The blind and bloody soldier with foul hand

Defile the locks of your shrill-shrieking daughters;
Your fathers taken by the silver beards,
And their most reverend heads dashed to the walls;
Your naked infants spitted upon pikes,
While the mad mothers with their howls confused
Do break the clouds, as did the wives of Jewry
At Herod's bloody-hunting slaughtermen.
What say you? Will you yield, and this avoid?
Or, guilty in defence, be thus destroyed?

Enter the Governor on the wall

GOVERNOR
Our expectation has this day an end.
The Dauphin, whom of succours we entreated,
Returns us that his forces are yet not ready
To raise so great a siege. Therefore, great King,
We yield our town and lives to your soft mercy.
Enter our gates, dispose of us and ours,
For we no longer are defensible.
KING HENRY
Open your gates.
                                      Exit Governor
            Come, uncle Exeter,
Go you and enter Harfleur; there remain,
And fortify it strongly against the French.
Use mercy to them all. For us, dear uncle,
The winter coming on, and sickness growing
Upon our soldiers, we will retire to Calais.
Tonight in Harfleur will we be your guest;
Tomorrow for the march are we addressed.

Flourish, and enter the town

SCENE IV[1]
Rouen. The palace.

Enter Katherine and Alice, an old gentlewoman

KATHERINE   Alice, tu as été en Angleterre, et tu parles
bien le langage.

ALICE   Un peu, madame.

KATHERINE   Je te prie, m'enseignez—il faut que j'apprenne
à parler. Comment appelez-vous la main en anglais?

ALICE   La main? Elle est appelée the hand.

KATHERINE   The hand. Et les doigts?

ALICE   Les doigts? Ma foi, j'oublie les doigts, mais je me
souviendrai. Les doigts? Je pense qu'ils sont appelés the
fingers; oui, the fingers.

KATHERINE   La main, the hand; les doigts, the fingers. Je
pense que je suis le bon écolier; j'ai gagné deux mots
d'anglais vitement. Comment appelez-vous les ongles?

ALICE   Les ongles? Nous les appelons the nails.

KATHERINE   The nails. Écoutez: dites-moi si je parle
bien—the hand, the fingers, et de nails.

ALICE   C'est bien dit, madame. Il est fort bon anglais.

KATHERINE   Dites-moi l'anglais pour le bras.

ALICE   The arm, madame.

KATHERINE   Et le coude?

ALICE   The elbow.

KATHERINE   The elbow. Je m'en fais la répétition de tous
les mots que vous m'avez appris dès à présent.

ALICE   Il est trop difficile, madame, comme je pense.

KATHERINE   Excusez-moi, Alice; écoutez—the hand, the
finger, the nails, the arm, the bilbow.

ALICE   The elbow, madame.

KATHERINE   O Seigneur Dieu, je m'en oublie! The elbow.
Comment appelez-vous le col?

---

[1]This scene is translated in the Appendix.

ALICE   The neck, madame.

KATHERINE   The neck. Et le menton?

ALICE   The chin.

KATHERINE   The chin. Le col, the neck; le menton, the chin.

ALICE   Oui. Sauf votre honneur, en vérité, vous prononcez les mots aussi droit que les natifs d'Angleterre.

KATHERINE   Je ne doute point d'apprendre, par la grace de Dieu, et en peu de temps.

ALICE   N'avez-vous pas déjà oublié ce que je vous ai enseigné?

KATHERINE   Non, je réciterai à vous promptement: the hand, the finger, the mails—

ALICE   The nails, madame.

KATHERINE   The nails, the arm, the ilbow—

ALICE   Sauf votre honneur, the elbow.

KATHERINE   Ainsi dis-je: the elbow, the neck, et the chin. Comment appelez-vous le pied et la robe?

ALICE   Le foot, madame, et le count.[2]

KATHERINE   Le foot, et le count? O Seigneur Dieu! Ils sont mots de son mauvais, corruptible, gros, et impudique, et non pour les dames d'honneur d'user. Je ne voudrais prononcer ces mots devant les seigneurs de France pour tout le monde. Foh! Le foot et le count! Néanmoins, je réciterai une autre fois ma leçon ensemble. The hand, the finger, the nails, the arm, the elbow, the neck, the chin, the foot, le count.

ALICE   Excellent, madame!

KATHERINE   C'est assez pour une fois. Allons-nous à dîner.   *Exeunt*

---

[2]Bawdy, of course.

SCENE V
The same.

Enter the King of France, the Dauphin,
the Duke of Brittany, the Constable of France,
and others

FRENCH KING

'Tis certain he has passed the River Somme.

CONSTABLE

And if he is not fought with now, my lord,
Let us not live in France: let us quit all,
And give our vineyards to a barbarous people.

DAUPHIN

O Dieu vivant![3] Shall a few sprays of us,
The emptying of our fathers' lustfulness,
Our scions, put in wild and savage stock,
Spirt up so suddenly into the clouds,
And overlook their grafters?

BRITTANY

Normans, but bastard Normans, Norman bastards!
Mort de ma vie![4] If they march along
Unfought with now, but I will sell my dukedom
To buy a sloppy and a dirty farm
In that crabbèd isle of Albion.

CONSTABLE

Dieu de batailles![5] Where have they this mettle?
Is not their climate foggy, raw, and dull,
On which, as in despite, the sun looks pale,
Killing their fruit with frowns? Can sodden water,

---

[3]O living God.
[4]Death of my life.
[5]God of battles.

A drench for over-reined jades, their barley broth,
Warm up their cold blood to such valiant heat?
And shall our quick blood, spirited with wine,
Seem frosty? O, for honour of our land,
Let us not hang like roping icicles
Upon our houses' thatch, while a more frosty people
Sweat drops of gallant youth in our rich fields!—
Poor we call them 'in their native lords.

DAUPHIN

By faith and honour,
Our madams mock at us, and plainly say
Our mettle is bred out, and they will give
Their bodies to the lust of English youth,
To new-store France with bastard warriors.

BRITAINE

They bid us to the English dancing-schools,
And teach lavoltas high and swift corantos,
Saying our grace is only in our heels,
And that we are most lofty runaways.

FRENCH KING

Where is Montjoy the Herald? Speed him hence,
Let him greet England with our sharp defiance.
Up, Princes, and with spirit of honour edged,
Sharper than your swords, hie to the field!
Charles Delabreth, High Constable of France,
You Dukes of Orleans, Bourbon, and of Berri,
Alençon, Brabant, Bar, and Burgundy,
Jaques Chatillon, Rambures, Vaudemont,
Beaumont, Grandpré, Roussi, and Faulconbridge,
Foix, Lestrake, Bouciqualt, and Charolois,
High Dukes, great Princes, Barons, Lords, and Knights,
For your great seats, now quit you of great shames.
Bar Harry England, that sweeps through our land
With pennons painted in the blood of Harfleur!
Rush on his host, as does the melted snow
Upon the valleys, whose low vassal seat

The Alps do spit and void their snot upon!
Go down upon him, you have power enough,
And in a captive chariot into Rouen
Bring him our prisoner.
CONSTABLE   This becomes the great.
Sorry am I his numbers are so few,
His soldiers sick, and famished in their march.
For I am sure, when he shall see our army,
He'll drop his heart into the sink of fear,
And for achievement offer us his ransom.
FRENCH KING
Therefore, Lord Constable, haste on Montjoy,
And let him say to England that we send
To know what willing ransom he will give.
Prince Dauphin, you shall stay with us in Rouen.
DAUPHIN
Not so, I do beseech your majesty.
FRENCH KING
Be patient, for you shall remain with us.
Now forth, Lord Constable, and Princes all,
And quickly bring us word of England's fall.   *Exeunt*

SCENE VI
The English camp.

Enter Captains Gower and Fluellen

GOWER   How now, Captain Fluellen? Come you from
the bridge?
FLUELLEN   I assure you, there is very excellent service
committed at the bridge.
GOWER   Is the Duke of Exeter safe?
FLUELLEN   The Duke of Exeter is as magnanimous as
Agamemnon, and a man that I love and honour with
my soul, and my heart, and my duty, and my life, and

my living, and my uttermost power. He has not—God
be praised and blessed!—any hurt in the world, but
keeps the bridge most valiantly, with excellent discipline.
There is an ancient lieutenant there at the bridge, I
think in my very conscience he is as valiant a man as
Mark Antony, and he is a man of no estimation in the
world, but I did see him do as gallant service.

GOWER   What do you call him?

FLUELLEN   He is called Ancient Pistol.

GOWER   I know him not.

Enter Pistol

FLUELLEN   Here is the man.

PISTOL

Captain, I you beseech to do me favours.

The Duke of Exeter does love you well.

FLUELLEN   Ay, I praise God, and I have merited some
love at his hands.

PISTOL

Bardolph, a soldier firm and sound of heart,

And of buxom valour, has, by cruel fate,

And giddy Fortune's furious fickle wheel,

That goddess blind,

That stands upon the rolling restless stone—

FLUELLEN   By your patience, Ancient Pistol: Fortune is
painted blind, with a muffler afore her eyes, to signify
to you that Fortune is blind. And she is painted also
with a wheel, to signify to you, which is the moral of it,
that she is turning, and inconstant, and mutability,
and variation; and her foot, look you, is fixed upon a
spherical stone, which rolls, and rolls, and rolls. In
good truth, the poet makes a most excellent description
of it. Fortune is an excellent moral.

PISTOL

> Fortune is Bardolph's foe, and frowns on him;
> For he has stolen a pax, and hangèd must he be—
> A damnèd death!
> Let gallows gape for dog; let man go free,
> And let not hemp his windpipe suffocate.
> But Exeter has given sentence of death
> For pax of little price.
> Therefore go speak—the Duke will hear your voice;
> And let not Bardolph's vital thread be cut
> With edge of penny cord and vile reproach.
> Speak, Captain, for his life, and I will you requite.

FLUELLEN   Ancient Pistol, I do partly understand your meaning.

PISTOL

> Why then, rejoice therefor!

FLUELLEN   Certainly, Ancient, it is not a thing to rejoice at, for if, look you, he was my brother, I would desire the Duke to use his good pleasure, and put him to execution; for discipline ought to be used.

PISTOL

> Die and be damned! and *figo* for your friendship.

FLUELLEN   It is well.

PISTOL

> The fig of Spain!   *Exit*

FLUELLEN   Very good.

GOWER   Why, this is an arrant counterfeit rascal, I remember him now—a pimp, a cutpurse.

FLUELLEN   I'll assure you, he uttered as brave words at the bridge as you shall see in a summer's day. But it is very well; what he has spoken to me, that is well, I warrant you, when time is served.

GOWER   Why, 'tis a gull, a fool, a rogue, that now and then goes to the wars, to grace himself at his return into London under the form of a soldier. And such fellows are perfect in the great commanders' names, and they

will teach you by rote where services were done. At such
and such a sconce, at such a breach, at such a convoy;
who came off bravely, who was shot, who disgraced,
what terms the enemy stood on. And this they learn
perfectly in the phrase of war, which they trick up with
new-tuned oaths. And what a beard of the general's cut
and a horrid suit of the camp will do among foaming
bottles and ale-washed wits is wonderful to be thought
of. But you must learn to know such slanders of the age,
or else you may be marvellously mistaken.

FLUELLEN   I tell you what, Captain Gower; I do perceive
he is not the man that he would gladly make show to
the world he is. If I find a hole in his coat, I will tell
him my mind.

(Drum within)

Hark you, the King is coming, and I must speak with
him from the bridge.

Drum and colours. Enter the King and soldiers,
with Gloucester

God bless your majesty!

KING HENRY
How now, Fluellen, came you from the bridge?

FLUELLEN   Ay, so please your majesty. The Duke of Exeter
has very gallantly maintained the bridge. The French is
gone off, look you, and there is gallant and most brave
passages. Indeed, the adversary was in possession of the
bridge, but he is enforced to retire, and the Duke of
Exeter is master of the bridge. I can tell your majesty,
the Duke is a brave man.

KING HENRY   What men have you lost, Fluellen?

FLUELLEN   The perdition of the adversary has been very
great, reasonable great. For my part, I think the Duke

has lost never a man, but one that is like to be executed
for robbing a church, one Bardolph, if your majesty
knows the man: his face is all bubbles and whelks, and
knobs, and flames of fire; and his lips blow at his nose,
and it is like a coal of fire, sometimes blue, and sometimes
red; but his nose is executed, and his fire is out.

KING HENRY   We would have all such offenders so cut
off. And we give express charge that in our marches
through the country there be nothing compelled from
the villages, nothing taken but paid for, none of the
French upbraided or abused in disdainful language. For
when lenity and cruelty play for a kingdom, the gentler
gamester is the soonest winner.

Tucket. Enter Montjoy

MONTJOY   You know me by my habit.

KING HENRY   Well then, I know you: what shall I know
of you?

MONTJOY   My master's mind.

KING HENRY   Unfold it.

MONTJOY   Thus says my King: 'Say you to Harry of
England, Though we seemed dead, we did but sleep.
Advantage is a better soldier than rashness. Tell him we
could have rebuked him at Harfleur, but that we thought
not good to bruise an injury till it was full ripe. Now we
speak upon our cue, and our voice is imperial: England
shall repent his folly, see his weakness, and admire our
sufferance. Bid him therefore consider of his ransom,
which must proportion the losses we have borne, the
subjects we have lost, the disgrace we have digested;
which in weight to re-answer, his pettiness would bow
under. For our losses, his exchequer is too poor; for the
effusion of our blood, the muster of his kingdom too
faint a number; and for our disgrace, his own person
kneeling at our feet but a weak and worthless satisfaction.

To this add defiance: and tell him for conclusion, he
has betrayed his followers, whose condemnation is
pronounced.' So far my King and master; so much my
office.

KING HENRY

What is your name? I know your quality.

MONTJOY   Montjoy.

KING HENRY

You do your office fairly. Turn you back,
And tell your King I do not seek him now,
But could be willing to march on to Calais
Without impeachment. For, to say the truth,
Though it is no wisdom to confess so much
Unto an enemy of craft and vantage,
My people are with sickness much enfeebled,
My numbers lessened, and those few I have
Almost no better than so many French—
Who when they were in health, I tell you Herald,
I thought upon one pair of English legs
Did march three Frenchmen. Yet forgive me, God,
That I do brag thus! This your air of France
Has blown that vice in me—I must repent.
Go, therefore, tell your master here I am;
My ransom is this frail and worthless trunk;
My army but a weak and sickly guard.
Yet, God before, tell him we will come on,
Though France himself, and such another neighbour,
Stand in our way. There's for your labour, Montjoy.
Go bid your master well advise himself:
If we may pass, we will; if we are hindered,
We shall your tawny ground with your red blood
Discolour. And so, Montjoy, fare you well.
The sum of all our answer is but this:
We would not seek a battle as we are,
Nor, as we are, we say we will not shun it.
So tell your master.

MONTJOY
  I shall deliver so. Thanks to your highness.   *Exit*
GLOUCESTER
  I hope they will not come upon us now.
KING HENRY
  We are in God's hand, brother, not in theirs.
  March to the bridge; it now draws toward night.
  Beyond the river we'll encamp ourselves,
  And on tomorrow bid them march away.

                                                      Exeunt

SCENE VII
The French camp.

*Enter the Constable of France, Rambures, Orleans,
Dauphin, with others*

CONSTABLE   Tut! I have the best armour of the world.
  Would it were day!
ORLEANS   You have an excellent armour; but let my
  horse have his due.
CONSTABLE   It is the best horse of Europe.
ORLEANS   Will it never be morning?
DAUPHIN   My Lord of Orleans, and my Lord High
  Constable, you talk of horse and armour?
ORLEANS   You are as well provided of both as any prince
  in the world.
DAUPHIN   What a long night is this! I will not change
  my horse with any that treads but on four pasterns. *Ça,
  ha!* He bounds from the earth as if his entrails were
  hairs—*le cheval volant,* the Pegasus, *chez les narines de
  feu!*[6] When I bestride him, I soar, I am a hawk. He
  trots the air; the earth sings when he touches it; the

---

[6]The flying horse, with nostrils of fire.

basest horn of his hoof is more musical than the pipe of
Hermes.

ORLEANS He's of the colour of the nutmeg.

DAUPHIN And of the heat of the ginger. It is a beast for
Perseus: he is pure air and fire; and the dull elements of
earth and water never appear in him, but only in patient
stillness while his rider mounts him. He is indeed a
horse, and all other jades you may call beasts.

CONSTABLE Indeed, my lord, it is a most absolute and
excellent horse.

DAUPHIN It is the prince of palfreys; his neigh is like the
bidding of a monarch, and his countenance enforces
homage.

ORLEANS No more, cousin.

DAUPHIN Nay, the man has no wit that cannot, from the
rising of the lark to the lodging of the lamb, vary
deserved praise on my palfrey. It is a theme as fluent as
the sea: turn the sands into eloquent tongues, and my
horse is argument for them all. It is a subject for a
sovereign to reason on, and for a sovereign's sovereign to
ride on; and for the world, familiar to us and unknown,
to lay apart their particular functions and wonder at
him. I once wrote a sonnet in his praise, and began thus:
'Wonder of nature—'.

ORLEANS I have heard a sonnet begin so to one's mistress.

DAUPHIN Then did they imitate that which I composed
to my courser, for my horse is my mistress.

ORLEANS Your mistress bears well.

DAUPHIN Me well, which is the prescript praise and
perfection of a good and particular mistress.

CONSTABLE Nay, for I thought yesterday your mistress
shrewdly shook your back.

DAUPHIN So perhaps did yours.

CONSTABLE Mine was not bridled.

DAUPHIN O, then perhaps she was old and gentle, and
you rode like a kern of Ireland, your French hose off,

and in your straight breeks.

CONSTABLE   You have good judgement in horsemanship.

DAUPHIN   Be warned by me, then: they that ride so, and
ride not warily, fall into foul bogs. I had rather have my
horse to my mistress.

CONSTABLE   I had as soon have my mistress a jade.

DAUPHIN   I tell you, Constable, my mistress wears his
own hair.

CONSTABLE   I could make as true a boast as that, if I had
a sow to my mistress.

DAUPHIN   *'Le chien est retourné à son propre vomissement,
et la truie lavée au bourbier':*[7] You make use of
anything.

CONSTABLE   Yet do I not use my horse for my mistress, or
any such proverb so little kin to the purpose.

RAMBURES   My Lord Constable, the armour that I saw in
your tent tonight—are those stars or suns upon it?

CONSTABLE   Stars, my lord.

DAUPHIN   Some of them will fall tomorrow, I hope.

CONSTABLE   And yet my sky shall not want.

DAUPHIN   That may be, for you bear many superfluously,
and it would be more honour some were away.

CONSTABLE   Even as your horse bears your praises, who
would trot as well were some of your brags dismounted.

DAUPHIN   Would I were able to load him with his desert!
Will it never be day? I will trot tomorrow a mile, and
my way shall be paved with English faces.

CONSTABLE   I will not say so, for fear I should be faced
out of my way; but I would it were morning, for I would
fain be about the ears of the English.

RAMBURES   Who will go to hazard with me for twenty
prisoners?

---

[7]The dog has returned to its own vomit, and the washed
sow to the mire.

CONSTABLE   You must first go yourself to hazard ere you
   have them.

DAUPHIN   'Tis midnight: I'll go arm myself.   *Exit*

ORLEANS   The Dauphin longs for morning.

RAMBURES   He longs to eat the English.

CONSTABLE   I think he will eat all he kills.

ORLEANS   By the white hand of my lady, he's a gallant
   prince.

CONSTABLE   Swear by her foot, that she may tread out the
   oath.

ORLEANS   He is simply the most active gentleman of
   France.

CONSTABLE   Doing is activity, and he will ever be doing.

ORLEANS   He never did harm, that I heard of.

CONSTABLE   And will do none tomorrow: he will keep
   that good name still.

ORLEANS   I know him to be valiant.

CONSTABLE   I was told that by one that knows him better
   than you.

ORLEANS   What's he?

CONSTABLE   Well, he told me so himself, and he said he
   cared not who knew it.

ORLEANS   He needs not; it is no hidden virtue in him.

CONSTABLE   By my faith, sir, but it is; never anybody
   saw it but his lackey. It is a hooded valour, and when it
   appears it will dwindle.

ORLEANS   Ill will never said well.

CONSTABLE   I will cap that proverb with 'There is flattery
   in friendship.'

ORLEANS   And I will take up that with 'Give the devil
   his due!'

CONSTABLE   Well placed! There stands your friend for
   the devil. Go for the very eye of that proverb with 'A pox
   on the devil!'

ORLEANS   You are the better at proverbs by how much 'A
   fool's bolt is soon shot.'

CONSTABLE   You have shot over.

ORLEANS   It is not the first time you were overshot.

Enter a Messenger

MESSENGER   My Lord High Constable, the English lie
within fifteen hundred paces of your tents.

CONSTABLE   Who has measured the ground?

MESSENGER   The Lord Grandpré.

CONSTABLE   A valiant and most expert gentleman. Would
it were day! Alas, poor Harry of England! He longs not
for the dawning as we do.

ORLEANS   What a wretched and peevish fellow is this
King of England, to mope with his fat-brained followers
so far out of his knowledge.

CONSTABLE   If the English had any apprehension they
would run away.

ORLEANS   That they lack; for if their heads had any
intellectual armour, they could never wear such heavy
head-pieces.

RAMBURES   That island of England breeds very valiant
creatures: their mastiffs are of unmatchable courage.

ORLEANS   Foolish curs, that run winking into the mouth
of a Russian bear, and have their heads crushed like
rotten apples! You may as well say that's a valiant flea
that dares eat his breakfast on the lip of a lion.

CONSTABLE   Just, just: and the men do sympathize with
the mastiffs in robustious and rough coming on, leaving
their wits with their wives. And then, give them great
meals of beef, and iron and steel; they will eat like
wolves, and fight like devils.

ORLEANS   Ay, but these English are sadly out of beef.

CONSTABLE   Then shall we find tomorrow they have only
stomachs to eat, and none to fight. Now is it time to
arm. Come, shall we about it?

ORLEANS
  It is now two o'clock: but, let me see—by ten
  We shall have each a hundred Englishmen.   *Exeunt*

Prologue to Act IV

Flourish. Enter Chorus

CHORUS
Now entertain conjecture of a time
When creeping murmur and the poring dark
Fill the wide vessel of the universe.
From camp to camp, through the foul womb of night,
The hum of either army stilly sounds,
That the fixed sentinels almost receive
The secret whispers of each other's watch.
Fire answers fire, and through their paly flames
Each army sees the other's umbered face.
Steed threatens steed, in high and boastful neighs,
Piercing the night's dull ear; and from the tents
The armourers, accomplishing the knights,
With busy hammers closing rivets up,
Give dreadful note of preparatiòn.
The country cocks do crow, the clocks do toll,
And the third hour of drowsy morning name.
Proud of their numbers, and secure in soul,
The confident and over-lusty French
Do the low-rated English play at dice,
And chide the cripple tardy-gaited night
Which like a foul and ugly witch does limp
So tediously away. The poor condemnèd English,
Like sacrifices, by their watchful fires
Sit patiently, and inly ruminate
The morning's danger. And their gesture sad,
Investing lank-lean cheeks and war-worn coats,
Presents them new unto the gazing moon
So many horrid ghosts. O now, who will behold

The royal Captain of this ruined band
Walking from watch to watch, from tent to tent,
Let him cry, 'Praise and glory on his head!'
For forth he goes and visits all his host,
Bids them good morrow with a modest smile,
And calls them brothers, friends, and countrymen.
Upon his royal face there is no note
How dread an army has enrounded him,
Nor does he dedicate one jot of colour
Unto the weary and all-watchèd night,
But freshly looks, and overbears discomfort
With cheerful semblance and sweet majesty;
That every wretch, pining and pale before,
Beholding him, plucks comfort from his looks.
A largess universal, like the sun,
His liberal eye does give to every one,
Thawing cold fear, that mean and gentle all
Behold, as may unworthiness define,
A little touch of Harry in the night.
And so our scene must to the battle fly;
Where—O for pity!—we shall much disgrace,
With four or five most vile and ragged foils,
Right ill-disposed in brawl ridiculous,
The name of Agincourt. Yet sit and see,
Minding true things by what their mockeries be.   *Exit*

Act IV

SCENE I
The English camp.

Enter the King, Bedford, and Gloucester

KING HENRY
Gloucester, 'tis true that we are in great danger:
The greater therefore should our courage be.
Good morrow, brother Bedford. God Almighty!
There is some soul of goodness in things evil,
Would men observingly distil it out;
For our bad neighbour makes us early stirrers,
Which is both healthful, and good husbandry.
Besides, they are our outward consciences,
And preachers to us all, admonishing
That we should dress us fairly for our end.
Thus may we gather honey from the weed,
And make a moral of the devil himself.

Enter Erpingham

Good morrow, old Sir Thomas Erpingham!
A good soft pillow for that good white head
Were better than a churlish turf of France.
ERPINGHAM
Not so, my liege—this lodging likes me better,
Since I may say, 'Now lie I like a king.'
KING HENRY
'Tis good for men to love their present pains
Upon example: so the spirit is eased;

And when the mind is quickened, out of doubt
The organs, though defunct and dead before,
Break up their drowsy grave and newly move
With cast-off slough and fresh legerity.
Lend me your cloak, Sir Thomas. Brothers both,
Commend me to the princes in our camp;
Do my good morrow to them, and anon
Desire them all to my paviliòn.

GLOUCESTER   We shall, my liege.

ERPINGHAM

Shall I attend your grace?

KING HENRY   No, my good knight.
Go with my brothers to my lords of England.
I and my bosom must debate awhile,
And then I would no other company.

ERPINGHAM

The Lord in heaven bless you, noble Harry!

Exeunt all but the King

KING HENRY

God-a-mercy, old heart, you speak cheerfully.

Enter Pistol

PISTOL

Qui va là? [Who goes there?]

KING HENRY   A friend.

PISTOL

Discuss unto me, are you officer,
Or are you base, common, and popular?

KING HENRY   I am a gentleman of a company.

PISTOL

Trail you the powerful pike?

KING HENRY   Even so. What are you?

PISTOL

As good a gentleman as the Emperor.

KING HENRY   Then you are a better than the King.

PISTOL

> The King's a good lad, and a heart of gold,
> A lad of life, an imp of fame;
> Of parents good, of fist most valiant.
> I kiss his dirty shoe, and from heartstring
> I love the lovely bully. What is your name?

KING HENRY   Harry le Roy.

PISTOL

> Le Roy? A Cornish name. Are you of Cornish crew?

KING HENRY   No, I am a Welshman.

PISTOL

> Know you Fluellen?

KING HENRY   Yes.

PISTOL

> Tell him I'll knock his leek about his pate
> Upon Saint Davy's day.

KING HENRY   Do not you wear your dagger in your cap
that day, lest he knock that about yours.

PISTOL

> Are you his friend?

KING HENRY   And his kinsman too.

PISTOL

> The *figo* for you then!

KING HENRY   I thank you. God be with you!

PISTOL

> My name is Pistol called.   *Exit*

KING HENRY   It sorts well with your fierceness.

Enter Fluellen and Gower

GOWER   Captain Fluellen!

FLUELLEN   So! In the name of Jesu Christ, speak lower. It
is the greatest admiration in the universal world, when
the true and ancient prerogatives and laws of the wars
are not kept. If you would take the pains but to examine
the wars of Pompey the Great, you shall find, I warrant

you, that there is no tiddle-taddle nor pibble-pabble in
Pompey's camp. I warrant you, you shall find the
ceremonies of the wars, and the cares of it, and the
forms of it, and the sobriety of it, and the modesty of it,
to be otherwise.

GOWER   Why, the enemy is loud, you hear him all night.

FLUELLEN   If the enemy is an ass, and a fool, and a
prating coxcomb, is it meet, think you, that we should
also, look you, be an ass, and a fool, and a prating
coxcomb? In your own conscience now?

GOWER   I will speak lower.

FLUELLEN   I pray you and beseech you that you will.

Exeunt Gower and Fluellen

KING HENRY

Though it appears a little out of fashion,

There are much care and valour in this Welshman.

*Enter three soldiers, John Bates, Alexander Court, and
Michael Williams*

COURT   Brother John Bates, is not that the morning which
breaks yonder?

BATES   I think it is; but we have no great cause to desire
the approach of day.

WILLIAMS   We see yonder the beginning of the day, but I
think we shall never see the end of it. Who goes there?

KING HENRY   A friend.

WILLIAMS   Under what captain serve you?

KING HENRY   Under Sir Thomas Erpingham.

WILLIAMS   A good old commander, and a most kind
gentleman. I pray you, what thinks he of our state?

KING HENRY   Even as men wrecked upon a sand, that
look to be washed off the next tide.

BATES   He has not told his thought to the King?

KING HENRY   No, nor is it meet he should. For though
I speak it to you, I think the King is but a man, as

I am. The violet smells to him as it does to me; the
element shows to him as it does to me; all his senses
have but human conditions. His ceremonies laid by, in
his nakedness he appears but a man; and though his
affections are higher mounted than ours, yet when they
stoop, they stoop with the like wing. Therefore, when
he sees reason of fears, as we do, his fears, out of doubt,
are of the same relish as ours are. Yet, in reason, no man
should possess him with any appearance of fear, lest he,
by showing it, should dishearten his army.

BATES   He may show what outward courage he will, but I
believe, as cold a night as it is, he could wish himself in
Thames up to the neck. And so I would he were, and I
by him, at all adventures, so we were quit here.

KING HENRY   By my word, I will speak my conscience of
the King: I think he would not wish himself anywhere
but where he is.

BATES   Then I would he were here alone; so should he be
sure to be ransomed, and many poor men's lives saved.

KING HENRY   I dare say you love him not so ill to wish
him here alone, howsoever you speak this to feel other
men's minds. I think I could not die anywhere so
contented as in the King's company, his cause being just
and his quarrel honourable.

WILLIAMS   That's more than we know.

BATES   Ay, or more than we should seek after; for we
know enough if we know we are the King's subjects. If
his cause is wrong, our obedience to the King wipes the
crime of it out of us.

WILLIAMS   But if the cause is not good, the King himself
has a heavy reckoning to make, when all those legs, and
arms, and heads, chopped off in a battle, shall join
together at the latter day, and cry all, 'We died at such a
place'. Some swearing, some crying for a surgeon; some
upon their wives left poor behind them, some upon the
debts they owe, some upon their children rawly left. I

am afraid there are few die well that die in a battle, for
how can they charitably dispose of anything when blood
is their argument? Now, if these men do not die well, it
will be a black matter for the King that led them to it,
whom to disobey were against all proportion of subjection.

KING HENRY   So, if a son that is by his father sent about
merchandise does sinfully miscarry upon the sea, the
imputation of his wickedness, by your rule, should
be imposed upon his father that sent him. Or if a
servant, under his master's command, transporting a
sum of money, is assailed by robbers, and dies in many
unreconciled iniquities, you may call the business of
the master the author of the servant's damnation. But
this is not so. The King is not bound to answer the
particular endings of his soldiers, the father of his son,
nor the master of his servant; for they purpose not their
death when they purpose their services. Besides, there is
no king, be his cause never so spotless, if it comes to the
arbitrament of swords, can try it out with all unspotted
soldiers. Some, peradventure, have on them the guilt of
premeditated and contrived murder; some, of beguiling
virgins with the broken seals of perjury; some, making
the wars their bulwark, that have before gored the
gentle bosom of peace with pillage and robbery. Now, if
these men have defeated the law, and outrun native
punishment, though they can outstrip men they have
no wings to fly from God. War is his beadle, war is his
vengeance; so that here men are punished for before-
breach of the King's laws, in now the King's quarrel.
Where they feared the death, they have borne life away;
and where they would be safe, they perish. Then if they
die unprepared, no more is the King guilty of their
damnation than he was before guilty of those impieties
for which they are now visited. Every subject's duty is
the King's, but every subject's soul is his own. Therefore
should every soldier in the wars do as every sick man in

his bed, wash every mote out of his conscience; and dying so, death is to him advantage. Or not dying, the time was blessedly lost wherein such preparation was gained; and in him that escapes, it were not sin to think that, making God so free an offer, he let him outlive that day to see his greatness, and to teach others how they should prepare.

WILLIAMS 'Tis certain, every man that dies ill, the ill upon his own head—the King is not to answer it.

BATES I do not desire he should answer for me, and yet I determine to fight lustily for him.

KING HENRY I myself heard the King say he would not be ransomed.

WILLIAMS Ay, he said so, to make us fight cheerfully: but when our throats are cut he may be ransomed, and we never the wiser.

KING HENRY If I live to see it, I will never trust his word after.

WILLIAMS You pay him out then! That's a perilous shot out of a pop-gun, that a poor and private displeasure can do against a monarch! You may as well go about to turn the sun to ice, with fanning in its face with a peacock's feather. You'll never trust his word after! Come, it is a foolish saying.

KING HENRY Your reproof is something too round. I should be angry with you, if the time was convenient.

WILLIAMS Let it be a quarrel between us, if you live.

KING HENRY I embrace it.

WILLIAMS How shall I know you again?

KING HENRY Give me any gage of yours and I will wear it in my bonnet. Then, if ever you dare acknowledge it, I will make it my quarrel.

WILLIAMS Here's my glove: give me another of yours.

KING HENRY There.

WILLIAMS This will I also wear in my cap. If ever you come to me and say, after tomorrow, 'This is my glove,' by this hand, I will give you a box on the ear.

KING HENRY   If ever I live to see it, I will challenge it.

WILLIAMS   You dare as well be hanged.

KING HENRY   Well, I will do it, though I take you in the
King's company.

WILLIAMS   Keep your word. Fare you well.

BATES   Be friends, you English fools, be friends! We have
French quarrels enough, if you could tell how to reckon.

KING HENRY   Indeed, the French may lay twenty French
crowns to one they will beat us, for they bear them on
their shoulders. But it is no English treason to cut
French crowns, and tomorrow the King himself will be
a clipper.   *Exeunt Soldiers*

Upon the King! Let us our lives, our souls,
Our debts, our careful wives,
Our children, and our sins, lay on the King!
We must bear all. O hard conditiòn,
Twin-born with greatness, subject to the breath
Of every fool, whose sense no more can feel
But his own wringing! What infinite heart's ease
Must kings neglect that private men enjoy!
And what have kings that privates have not too,
Save ceremony, save general ceremony?
And what are you, you idol ceremony?
What kind of god are you, that suffer more
Of mortal griefs than do your worshippers?
What are your rents? What are your comings-in?
O ceremony, show me but your worth!
What is your soul of adoratiòn?
Are you aught else but place, degree, and form,
Creating awe and fear in other men?
Wherein you are less happy, being feared,
Than they in fearing.
What drink you oft, instead of homage sweet,
But poisoned flattery? O, be sick, great greatness,
And bid your ceremony give you cure!

Think you the fiery fever will go out
With titles blown from adulatiòn?
Will it give place to bowing and low bending?
Can you, when you command the beggar's knee,
Command the health of it? No, you proud dream,
That play so subtly with a king's repose.
I am a king that find you, and I know
It is not the balm, the sceptre, and the ball,
The sword, the mace, the crown imperial,
The intertissued robe of gold and pearl,
The stuffed title running before the king,
The throne he sits on, nor the tide of pomp
That beats upon the high shore of this world—
No, not all these, thrice-gorgeous ceremony,
Not all these, laid in bed majestical,
Can sleep so soundly as the wretched slave,
Who, with a body filled, and vacant mind,
Gets him to rest, crammed with distressful bread;
Never sees horrid night, the child of hell,
But, like a lackey, from the rise to set,
Sweats in the eye of Phoebus, and all night
Sleeps in Elysium. Next day after dawn
Does rise and help Hyperion to his horse;
And follows so the ever-running year
With profitable labour to his grave.
And but for ceremony, such a wretch,
Winding up days with toil, and nights with sleep,
Had the fore-hand and vantage of a king.
The slave, a member of the country's peace,
Enjoys it, but in gross brain little knows
What watch the king keeps to maintain the peace,
Whose hours the peasant best advantages.

Enter Erpingham

ERPINGHAM
    My lord, your nobles, suspicious of your absence,
    Seek through your camp to find you.
KING HENRY   Good old knight,
    Collect them all together at my tent.
    I'll be before you.
ERPINGHAM   I shall do it, my lord.   *Exit*
KING HENRY
    O God of battles, steel my soldiers' hearts;
    Possess them not with fear; take from them now
    The sense of reckoning, if the opposèd numbers
    Pluck their hearts from them. Not today, O Lord,
    O not today, think not upon the fault
    My father made in compassing the crown!
    I Richard's body have interrèd new,
    And on it have bestowed more contrite tears
    Than from it issued forcèd drops of blood.
    Five hundred poor I have in yearly pay,
    Who twice a day their withered hands hold up
    Toward heaven, to pardon blood. And I have built
    Two chantries where the sad and solemn priests
    Sing still for Richard's soul. More will I do,
    Though all that I can do is nothing worth,
    Since my penitence comes after all,
    Imploring pardon.

Enter Gloucester

GLOUCESTER
    My liege!
KING HENRY   My brother Gloucester's voice? Ay,
    I know your errand, I will go with thee.
    The day, my friends, and all things stay for me.
                            Exeunt

SCENE II
The French camp.

Enter the Dauphin, Orleans, Rambures, and others

ORLEANS
  The sun does gild our armour: up, my lords!
DAUPHIN
  Montez à cheval! My horse! Varlet! Lacquais![1]
  Ha!
ORLEANS
    O brave spirit!
DAUPHIN   *Via! Les eaux et la terre!*[2]
ORLEANS
  Rien plus? L'air et le feu?[3]
DAUPHIN   *Ciel,*[4] *cousin Orleans!*

Enter the Constable

  Now, my Lord Constable!
CONSTABLE
  Hark how our steeds for present service neigh!
DAUPHIN
  Mount them and make incision in their hides,
  That their hot blood may spin in English eyes
  And blind them with superfluous courage, ha!
RAMBURES
  What, will you have them weep our horses' blood?
  How shall we then behold their natural tears?

---

[1]Mount your horse. Groom! Lackey!
[2]Water and land.
[3]Nothing more? Air and fire.
[4]Sky.

Enter a Messenger

MESSENGER
  The English are embattled, you French peers.
CONSTABLE
  To horse, you gallant Princes, straight to horse!
  Do but behold yon poor and starvèd band,
  And your fair show shall suck away their souls,
  Leaving them but the shales and husks of men.
  There is not work enough for all our hands,
  Scarce blood enough in all their sickly veins
  To give each naked cutlass then a stain
  That our French gallants shall today draw out,
  And sheathe for lack of sport. Let us but blow on them,
  The vapour of our valour will o'erturn them.
  'Tis positive against all exceptions, lords,
  That our superfluous lackeys, and our peasants,
  Who in unnecessary action swarm
  About our squares of battle, were enough
  To purge this field of such a wretched foe,
  Though we upon this mountain's basis by
  Took stand for idle speculatiòn:
  But that our honours must not. What's to say?
  A very little little let us do,
  And all is done. Then let the trumpets sound
  The signal flourish and the note to mount;
  For our approach shall so much dare the field
  That England shall couch down in fear and yield.

Enter Grandpré

GRANDPRÉ
  Why do you stay so long, my lords of France?
  Yon island carrions, desperate of their bones,
  Ill-favouredly become the morning field.
  Their ragged banners poorly are let loose,

And our air shakes them passing scornfully.
Big Mars seems bankrupt in their beggared host,
And faintly through a rusty helmet peeps.
The horsemen sit like fixèd candlesticks,
With torch-staves in their hand; and their poor jades
Droop down their heads, dropping the hides and hips,
The gum down-roping from their pale-dead eyes;
And in their pale dull mouths the jointed bit
Lies foul with chewed grass, still and motionless.
And their executors, the knavish crows,
Fly over them all, impatient for their hour.
Description cannot suit itself in words
To demonstrate the life of such a battle
In life so lifeless as it shows itself.

CONSTABLE
They have said their prayers, and they stay for death.

DAUPHIN
Shall we go send them dinners, and fresh suits,
And give their fasting horses provender,
And after fight with them?

CONSTABLE
I stay but for my pennant. To the field!
I will the banner from a trumpeter take,
And use it for my haste. Come, come away!
The sun is high, and we outwear the day.   *Exeunt*

SCENE III
The English camp.

Enter Gloucester, Bedford, Exeter, Erpingham,
Salisbury and Westmorland, with soldiers

GLOUCESTER
  Where is the King?
BEDFORD
  The King himself has gone to view their army.
WESTMORLAND
  Of fighting men they have full three-score thousand.
EXETER
  There's five to one: besides, they all are fresh.
SALISBURY
  God's arm strike with us! It is a fearful odds.
  Good-bye you, Princes all: I'll to my charge.
  If we no more meet till we meet in heaven,
  Then joyfully, my noble Lord of Bedford,
  My dear Lord Gloucester, and my good Lord Exeter,
  And my kind kinsman, warriors all, adieu!
BEDFORD
  Farewell, good Salisbury, and good luck go with you!
EXETER
  Farewell, kind lord: fight valiantly today—
  And yet I do you wrong to mind you of it,
  For you are framed of the firm truth of valour.

                                        Exit Salisbury

BEDFORD
  He is as full of valour as of kindness,
  Princely in both.

                    Enter the King

WESTMORLAND   O that we now had here
  But one ten thousand of those men in England
  That do no work today!
KING HENRY   What's he that wishes so?
  My cousin Westmorland? No, my fair cousin.
  If we are marked to die, we are enough
  To do our country loss: and if to live,

The fewer men, the greater share of honour.
God's will! I pray you wish not one man more.
By Jove, I am not covetous for gold,
Nor care I who does feed upon my cost;
It grieves me not if men my garments wear;
Such outward things dwell not in my desires.
But if it is a sin to covet honour,
I am the most offending soul alive.
No, faith, cousin, wish not a man from England:
God's peace! I would not lose so great an honour
As one man more I think would share from me
For the best hope I have. O, do not wish one more!
Rather proclaim it, Westmorland, through my host,
That he who has no stomach to this fight,
Let him depart: his passport shall be made,
And crowns for convoy put into his purse.
We would not die in that man's company
That fears his fellowship to die with us.
This day is called the Feast of Crispian:
He that outlives this day, and comes safe home,
Will stand a-tiptoe when this day is named,
And rouse him at the name of Crispian.
He that shall see this day, and live old age,
Will yearly on the vigil feast his neighbours,
And say, 'Tomorrow is Saint Crispian.'
Then will he strip his sleeve, and show his scars,
And say, 'These wounds I had on Crispin's day.'
Old men forget; when all shall be forgotten
But he'll remember, with advantages,
What feats he did that day. Then shall our names,
Familiar in his mouth as household words,
Harry the King, Bedford and Exeter,
Warwick and Talbot, Salisbury and Gloucester,
Be in their flowing cups freshly remembered.
This story shall the good man teach his son;
And Crispin Crispian shall never go by,

From this day to the ending of the world,
But we in it shall be rememberèd —
We few, we happy few, we band of brothers.
For he today that sheds his blood with me
Shall be my brother; be he never so vile,
This day shall gentle his conditiòn;
And gentlemen in England now abed
Shall think themselves accursed they were not here,
And hold their manhoods cheap, while any speaks
That fought with us upon Saint Crispin's day.

Enter Salisbury

SALISBURY
My sovereign lord, bestow yourself with speed.
The French are bravely in their order set,
And will with all expedition charge on us.
KING HENRY
All things are ready, if our minds are so.
WESTMORLAND
Perish the man whose mind is backward now!
KING HENRY
You do not wish more help from England, cousin?
WESTMORLAND
God's will, my liege, would you and I alone,
Without more help, could fight this royal battle!
KING HENRY
Why, now you have unwished five thousand men,
Which likes me better than to wish us one.
You know your places. God be with you all!

Tucket. Enter Montjoy

MONTJOY
Once more I come to know of you, King Harry,
If for your ransom you will now compound,

Before your most assurèd overthrow:
For certainly you are so near the gulf
You needs must be swallowed. Besides, in mercy,
The Constable desires that you will mind
Your followers of repentance, that their souls
May make a peaceful and a sweet retreat
From off these fields, where, wretches, their poor bodies
Must lie and fester.

KING HENRY   Who has sent you now?

MONTJOY

The Constable of France.

KING HENRY

I pray you bear my former answer back:
Bid them achieve me, and then sell my bones.
Good God, why should they mock poor fellows thus?
The man that once did sell the lion's skin
While the beast lived, was killed in hunting him.
Many of our bodies shall no doubt
Find native graves; upon which then, I trust,
Shall witness live in brass of this day's work.
And those that leave their valiant bones in France,
Dying like men, though buried in your dunghills,
They shall be famed. For there the sun shall greet them,
And draw their honours reeking up to heaven,
Leaving their earthly parts to choke your clime,
The smell whereof shall breed a plague in France.
Mark then abounding valour in our English,
That being dead, like to the bullet's crashing,
Break out into a second course of mischief,
Killing in rebound of mortality.
Let me speak proudly: tell the Constable
We are but warriors for the working-day;
Our gayness and our gilt are all besmirched
With rainy marching in the painful field.
There's not a piece of feather in our host—
Good argument, I hope, we will not fly—

And time has worn us into slovenry.
But, by the mass, our hearts are in the trim;
And my poor soldiers tell me, yet ere night
They'll be in fresher robes, or they will pluck
The gay new coats o'er the French soldiers' heads,
And turn them out of service. If they do this—
As, if God please, they shall—my ransom then
Will soon be levied. Herald, save you your labour;
Come you no more for ransom, gentle Herald.
They shall have none, I swear, but these my joints,
Which if they have as I will leave 'em them
Shall yield them little, tell the Constable.

MONTJOY
I shall, King Harry. And so fare you well:
You never shall hear herald any more.   *Exit*

KING HENRY
I fear you will once more come again for a ransom.

Enter York

YORK
My lord, most humbly on my knee I beg
The leading of the vanguard.

KING HENRY
Take it, brave York. Now, soldiers, march away:
And how you please, God, then dispose the day!
                                                         Exeunt

SCENE IV
The battle-field.

Alarum. Excursions. Enter Pistol, French Soldier, Boy

PISTOL

Yield, cur!

FRENCH SOLDIER   *Je pense que vous êtes le gentilhomme*
de bonne qualité.[5]

PISTOL

Calitie! 'Calen o custure me!'

Are you a gentleman? What is your name? Discuss.

FRENCH SOLDIER   *O Seigneur Dieu!* [O, Lord God!]

PISTOL

O Signieur Dew should be a gentleman:

Consider my words, O Signieur Dew, and mark.

O Signieur Dew, you die on point of fox,

Except, O Signieur, you do give to me

Egregious ransom.

FRENCH SOLDIER   *O, prenez miséricorde! Ayez pitié de*
moy![6]

PISTOL

Moy shall not serve: I will have forty moys,

For I will fetch your rim out at your throat

In drops of crimson blood!

FRENCH SOLDIER   *Est-il impossible d'échapper la force de*
ton bras?[7]

PISTOL

Brass, cur?

You damnèd and most lustful mountain goat,

Offer me brass?

FRENCH SOLDIER   *O, pardonne-moy!* [Pardon me.]

PISTOL

Say you me so? Is that a ton of moys?

Come hither, boy: ask me this slave in French

What is his name.

---

[5] I think that you are a gentleman of quality.

[6] Have mercy! Have pity on me!

[7] Is it impossible to escape the force of your arm?

BOY   *Écoutez: comment êtes-vous appelé?* [Hark: what
    are you called?]

FRENCH SOLDIER   *Monsieur le Fer.*

BOY   He says his name is Master Fer.

PISTOL   Master Fer! I'll fer him, and firk him, and ferret
    him. Discuss the same in French unto him.

BOY   I do not know the French for fer, and ferret, and
    firk.

PISTOL

    Bid him prepare, for I will cut his throat.

FRENCH SOLDIER   *Que dit-il, monsieur?*

BOY   *Il me commande à vous dire que vous faites vous
    prêt, car ce soldat içi est disposé tout à cette heure de
    couper votre gorge.*[8]

PISTOL

    Owy, cuppele gorge, permafoy,

    Peasant, unless you give me crowns, brave crowns;

    Or mangled shall you be by this my sword.

FRENCH SOLDIER   *O, je vous supplie, pour l'amour de
    Dieu, me pardonner! Je suis le gentilhomme de bonne
    maison. Gardez ma vie, et je vous donnerai deux cents
    écus.*

PISTOL

    What are his words?

BOY   He prays you to save his life. He is a gentleman of a
    good house, and for his ransom he will give you two
    hundred crowns.

PISTOL

    Tell him my fury shall abate, and I

    The crowns will take.

FRENCH SOLDIER   *Petit monsieur, que dit-il?*

BOY   *Encore qu'il est contre son jurement de pardonner
    aucun prisonnier; néanmoins, pour les écus que vous*

---

[8]What does he say, sir? He bids me say prepare yourself,
for this soldier here is disposed to cut your throat at once.

*l'avez promis, il est content à vous donner la liberté, le
franchisement.*[9]

FRENCH SOLDIER   *Sur mes genoux je vous donne mille
remercîments; et je m'estime heureux que je suis tombé
entre les mains d'un chevalier, je pense, le plus brave,
vaillant, et très distingué seigneur d'Angleterre.*

PISTOL

Expound unto me, boy.

BOY   He gives you upon his knees a thousand thanks;
and he esteems himself happy that he has fallen into
the hands of one—as he thinks—the most brave, valorous,
and thrice-worthy signieur of England.

PISTOL

As I suck blood, I will some mercy show.

Follow me!   *Exit*

BOY   *Suivez-vous le grand capitaine.*

(Exit French Soldier)

I did never know so full a voice issue from so empty a
heart; but the saying is true, 'The empty vessel makes
the greatest sound.' Bardolph and Nym had ten times
more valour than this roaring devil in the old play,
that everyone may pare his nails with a wooden dagger.
They are both hanged—and so would this be, if he
durst steal anything adventurously. I must stay with
the lackeys, with the luggage of our camp. The French
might have a good prey of us, if he knew of it, for
there is none to guard it but boys.

Exit

---

[9]Although it is against his oath to grant pardon to any prisoner,
nevertheless for the crowns you have promised he is content to
give you liberty, freely.

SCENE V
The same.

Enter the Constable, Orleans, Bourbon, Dauphin,
and Rambures

CONSTABLE   *O diable!* [O, the devil!]
ORLEANS   *O Seigneur! Le jour est perdu, tout est perdu!*
[O Lord, the day is lost, all is lost!]
DAUPHIN
   Mort de ma vie! All is confounded, all!
   Reproach and everlasting shame
   Sits mocking in our plumes. *O méchante fortune!* [O ill
      fortune!]

A short alarum

   Do not run away!
CONSTABLE   Why, all our ranks are broken.
DAUPHIN
   O pèrdurable shame! Let's stab ourselves.
   Are these the wretches that we played at dice for?
ORLEANS
   Is this the King we sent to for his ransom?
BOURBON
   Shame, and eternal shame, nothing but shame!
   Let's die in honour! Once more back again!
   And he that will not follow Bourbon now,
   Let him go hence, and with his cap in hand,
   Like a base pander, hold the chamber-door
   While by a slave, no gentler than my dog,
   His fairest daughter is contaminated.
CONSTABLE
   Disorder that has spoiled us, friend us now!
   Let us on heaps go offer up our lives.

ORLEANS
    We are enough yet living in the field
    To smother up the English in our throngs,
    If any order might be thought upon.
BOURBON
    The devil take order now! I'll to the throng.
    Let life be short, else shame will be too long.   *Exeunt*

SCENE VI
The same.

Alarum. Enter the King and his train, Exeter and others,
with prisoners

KING HENRY
    Well have we done, thrice-valiant countrymen;
    But all's not done—yet keep the French the field.
EXETER
    The Duke of York commends him to your majesty.
KING HENRY
    Lives he, good uncle? Thrice within this hour
    I saw him down; thrice up again, and fighting.
    From helmet to the spur all blood he was.
EXETER
    In which array, brave soldier, does he lie,
    Larding the plain; and by his bloody side,
    Yoke-fellow to his honour-owning wounds,
    The noble Earl of Suffolk also lies.
    Suffolk first died; and York, hacked all over,
    Comes to him, where in gore he lay insteeped,
    And takes him by the beard, kisses the gashes
    That bloodily did yawn upon his face.
    He cries aloud, 'Tarry, my cousin Suffolk!
    My soul shall yours keep company to heaven.
    Tarry, sweet soul, for mine, then fly abreast,

As in this glorious and well-fought field
We kept together in our chivalry!'
Upon these words I came and cheered him up;
He smiled to me in the face, reached me his hand,
And, with a feeble grip, says, 'Dear my lord,
Commend my service to my sovereign.'
So did he turn, and over Suffolk's neck
He threw his wounded arm, and kissed his lips,
And so espoused to death, with blood he sealed
A testament of noble-ending love.
The pretty and sweet manner of it forced
Those waters from me which I would have stopped;
But I had not so much of man in me,
And all my mother came into my eyes
And gave me up to tears.

KING HENRY   I blame you not;
For, hearing this, I must perforce compound
With mistful eyes, or they will issue too.

Alarum

But hark! what new alarum is this same?
The French have reinforced their scattered men.
Then every soldier kill his prisoners!
Give the word through.   *Exeunt*

SCENE VII
The same.

Enter Fluellen and Gower

FLUELLEN   Kill the boys and the luggage? 'Tis expressly
against the law of arms; 'tis as arrant a piece of knavery,
mark you now, as can be offert—in your conscience
now, is it not?

GOWER   'Tis certain there's not a boy left alive, and the cowardly rascals that ran from the battle have done this slaughter. Besides, they have burnt and carried away all that was in the King's tent, wherefore the King most worthily has caused every soldier to cut his prisoner's throat. O, 'tis a gallant King!

FLUELLEN   Ay, he was born at Monmouth, Captain Gower. What call you the town's name where Alexander the Big was born?

GOWER   Alexander the Great.

FLUELLEN   Why, I pray you, is not 'big' great? The big, or the great, or the mighty, or the huge, or the magnanimous, are all one reckoning, save the phrase is a little variations.

GOWER   I think Alexander the Great was born in Macedon; his father was called Philip of Macedon, as I take it.

FLUELLEN   I think it is in Macedon where Alexander is born. I tell you, Captain, if you look in the maps of the world, I warrant you shall find, in the comparison between Macedon and Monmouth, that the situation, look you, is both alike. There is a river in Macedon, and there is also moreover a river at Monmouth—it is called Wye at Monmouth, but it is out of my brains what is the name of the other river; but 'tis all one, 'tis alike as my fingers is to my fingers, and there is salmon in both. If you mark Alexander's life well, Harry of Monmouth's· life comes after it indifferent well; for there is figures in all things. Alexander, God knows and you know, in his rages, and his furies, and his wraths, and his cholers, and his moods, and his displeasures, and his indignations, and also being a little intoxicated in his brains, did in his ales and his angers, look you, kill his best friend Cleitus.

GOWER   Our King is not like him in that: he never killed any of his friends.

FLUELLEN   It is not well done, mark you now, to take the
tales out of my mouth, ere it is made and finished. I speak
but in the figure and comparison of it. As Alexander
killed his friend Cleitus, being in his ales and his cups,
so also Harry Monmouth, being in his right wits and
his good judgement, turned away the fat knight with
the great-belly doublet—he was full of jests, and gibes,
and knaveries, and mocks: I have forgot his name.

GOWER   Sir John Falstaff.

FLUELLEN   That is he. I'll tell you, there is good men born
at Monmouth.

GOWER   Here comes his majesty.

*Alarum. Enter King Henry and Bourbon, with prisoners;
also Warwick, Gloucester, Exeter, and others. Flourish*

KING HENRY
I was not angry since I came to France
Until this instant. Take a trumpet, Herald;
Ride you unto the horsemen on yon hill.
If they will fight with us, bid them come down,
Or void the field: they do offend our sight.
If they'll do neither, we will come to them,
And make them scurry away as swift as stones
Enforcèd from the old Assyrian slings.
Besides, we'll cut the throats of those we have,
And not a man of them that we shall take
Shall taste our mercy. Go and tell them so.

Enter Montjoy

EXETER
Here comes the Herald of the French, my liege.

GLOUCESTER
His eyes are humbler than they used to be.

KING HENRY
    How now, what means this, Herald? Know you not
    That I have fined these bones of mine for ransom?
    Come you again for ransom?
MONTJOY   No, great King;
    I come to you for charitable licence,
    That we may wander over this bloody field
    To book our dead, and then to bury them,
    To sort our nobles from our common men.
    For many of our princes—woe the while!—
    Lie drowned and soaked in mercenary blood.
    So do our vulgar drench their peasant limbs
    In blood of princes, and their wounded steeds
    Struggle fetlock-deep in gore, and with wild rage
    Yerk out their armèd heels at their dead masters,
    Killing them twice. O, give us leave, great King,
    To view the field in safety, and dispose
    Of their dead bodies!
KING HENRY   I tell you truly, Herald,
    I know not if the day is ours or no;
    For yet many of your horsemen do peer
    And gallop over the field.
MONTJOY   The day is yours.
KING HENRY
    Praisèd be God, and not our strength, for it!
    What is this castle called that stands hard by?
MONTJOY
    They call it Agincourt.
KING HENRY
    Then call we this the field of Agincourt,
    Fought on the day of Crispin Crispian.
FLUELLEN   Your grandfather of famous memory, if it please
your majesty, and your great-uncle Edward the Black
Prince of Wales, as I have read in the chronicles, fought
a most brave battle here in France.

KING HENRY   They did, Fluellen.

FLUELLEN   Your majesty says very true. If your majesty is
    remembered of it, the Welshmen did good service in a
    garden where leeks did grow, wearing leeks in their
    Monmouth caps, which your majesty knows to this
    hour is an honourable badge of the service; and I do
    believe your majesty takes no scorn to wear the leek
    upon Saint Davy's day.

KING HENRY

    I wear it for a memorable honour;
    For I am Welsh, you know, good countryman.

FLUELLEN   All the water in Wye cannot wash your majesty's
    Welsh blood out of your body, I can tell you that. God
    bless it and preserve it, as long as it pleases his grace,
    and his majesty too!

KING HENRY   Thanks, good my countryman.

FLUELLEN   By Jesu, I am your majesty's countryman, I
    care not who knows it; I will confess it to all the world. I
    need not to be ashamed of your majesty, praised be God,
    so long as your majesty is an honest man.

KING HENRY

    God keep me so!

Enter Williams

    Our heralds go with him.
    Bring me just notice of the numbers dead
    On both our parts.   *Exeunt Heralds with Montjoy*
                    Call yonder fellow hither.

EXETER   Soldier, you must come to the King.

KING HENRY   Soldier, why wear you that glove in your
    cap?

WILLIAMS   If it please your majesty, it is the gage of one
    that I should fight with, if he is alive.

KING HENRY   An Englishman?

WILLIAMS If it please your majesty, a rascal that swaggered
     with me last night: who, if he lives and ever dares to
     challenge this glove, I have sworn to take him a box on
     the ear. Or if I can see my glove in his cap, which he
     swore as he was a soldier he would wear if alive, I will
     strike it out soundly.

KING HENRY What think you, Captain Fluellen, is it fit
     this soldier should keep his oath?

FLUELLEN He is a craven and a villain else, if it please
     your majesty, in my conscience.

KING HENRY It may be his enemy is a gentleman of great
     sort, quite from the answer of his degree.

FLUELLEN Though he is as good a gentleman as the devil
     is, as Lucifer and Belzebub himself, it is necessary, look
     your grace, that he should keep his vow and his oath. If
     he is perjured, see you now, his reputation is as arrant a
     villain and a saucy knave as ever his black shoe trod
     upon God's ground and his earth, in my conscience, la!

KING HENRY Then keep your vow, man, when you meet
     the fellow.

WILLIAMS So I will, my liege, as I live.

KING HENRY Whom serve you under?

WILLIAMS Under Captain Gower, my liege.

FLUELLEN Gower is a good captain, and is good knowledge
     and literatured in the wars.

KING HENRY Call him hither to me, soldier.

WILLIAMS I will, my liege.   *Exit*

KING HENRY Here, Fluellen, wear you this favour for me,
     and stick it in your cap. When Alençon and myself were
     down together, I plucked this glove from his helm. If
     any man challenges this, he is a friend to Alençon, and
     an enemy to our person: if you encounter any such,
     apprehend him, if you do me love.

FLUELLEN Your grace does me as great honour as can be
     desired in the hearts of his subjects. I would fain see the
     man that has but two legs that shall find himself

aggrieved at this glove, that is all: but I would fain see it
once, and please God of his grace that I might see.

KING HENRY   Know you Gower?

FLUELLEN   He is my dear friend, please you.

KING HENRY   Pray go seek him, and bring him to my
tent.

FLUELLEN   I will fetch him.   *Exit*

KING HENRY
My Lord of Warwick, and my brother Gloucester,
Follow Fluellen closely at the heels.
The glove which I have given him for a favour
May haply purchase him a box on the ear.
It is the soldier's: I by bargain should
Wear it myself. Follow, good cousin Warwick.
If the soldier strikes him, as I judge
By his blunt bearing he will keep his word,
Some sudden mischief may arise of it.
For I do know Fluellen valiant,
And, touched with choler, hot as gunpowder,
And quickly will return an injury.
Follow, and see there is no harm between them.
Go you with me, uncle of Exeter.   *Exeunt*

SCENE VIII
Before King Henry's pavilion.

Enter Gower and Williams

WILLIAMS   I warrant it is to knight you, Captain.

Enter Fluellen

FLUELLEN   God's will and his pleasure, Captain, I beseech
you now, come apace to the King. There is more good
toward you, peradventure, than is in your knowledge to
dream of.

WILLIAMS   Sir, know you this glove?

FLUELLEN   Know the glove? I know the glove is a glove.

WILLIAMS   I know this; and thus I challenge it.

He strikes him

FLUELLEN   'Sblood! an arrant traitor as any's in the universal world, or in France, or in England!

GOWER   How now, sir? You villain!

WILLIAMS   Do you think I'll be denied?

FLUELLEN   Stand away, Captain Gower: I will give treason his payment into blows, I warrant you.

WILLIAMS   I am no traitor.

FLUELLEN   That's a lie in your throat. I charge you in his majesty's name, apprehend him: he's a friend of the Duke Alençon's.

Enter Warwick and Gloucester

WARWICK   How now, how now, what's the matter?

FLUELLEN   My Lord of Warwick, here is—praised be God for it!—a most contagious treason come to light, look you, as you shall desire in a summer's day. Here is his majesty.

Enter the King and Exeter

KING HENRY   How now, what's the matter?

FLUELLEN   My liege, here is a villain and a traitor, that, look your grace, has struck the glove which your majesty took out of the helmet of Alençon.

WILLIAMS   My liege, this was my glove, here is the fellow of it; and he that I gave it to in change promised to wear it in his cap. I promised to strike him if he did. I met this man with my glove in his cap, and I have been as good as my word.

FLUELLEN   Your majesty hear now, saving your majesty's
   manhood, what an arrant, rascally, beggarly, lousy knave
   it is. I hope your majesty bears me testimony and witness,
   and will avouch, that this is the glove of Alençon that
   your majesty gave me, in your conscience, now.

KING HENRY   Give me your glove, soldier. Look, here is
   the fellow of it.
   It was I indeed you promised to strike,
   And you have given me most bitter terms.

FLUELLEN   Please your majesty, let his neck answer for it,
   if there is any martial law in the world.

KING HENRY   How can you make me satisfaction?

WILLIAMS   All offences, my lord, come from the heart:
   never came any from mine that might offend your
   majesty.

KING HENRY   It was ourself you did abuse.

WILLIAMS   Your majesty came not like yourself: you
   appeared to me but as a common man—witness the
   night, your garments, your lowliness. And what your
   highness suffered under that shape, I beseech you take
   it for your own fault, and not mine; for had you been as
   I took you for, I made no offence. Therefore, I beseech
   your highness, pardon me.

KING HENRY
   Here, uncle Exeter, fill this glove with crowns,
   And give it to this fellow. Keep it, fellow,
   And wear it for an honour in your cap
   Till I do challenge it. Give him the crowns;
   And, Captain, you must needs be friends with him.

FLUELLEN   By this day and this light, the fellow has
   mettle enough in his belly. Hold, there is twelve pence
   for you, and I pray you to serve God, and keep you out of
   brawls, and brabbles, and quarrels, and dissensions,
   and I warrant you it is the better for you.

WILLIAMS   I will none of your money.

FLUELLEN   It is with a good will: I can tell you it will
    serve you to mend your shoes. Come, wherefore should
    you be so bashful?—your shoes are not so good; 'tis a
    good shilling, I warrant you, or I will change it.

Enter an English Herald

KING HENRY   Now, Herald, are the dead numbered?
HERALD
    Here is the number of the slaughtered French.

He gives him a paper

KING HENRY
    What prisoners of good sort are taken, uncle?
EXETER
    Charles Duke of Orleans, nephew to the King;
    John Duke of Bourbon, and Lord Bouciqualt;
    Of other lords and barons, knights and squires,
    Full fifteen hundred, besides common men.
KING HENRY
    This note does tell me of ten thousand French
    That in the field lie slain. Of princes, in this number,
    And nobles bearing banners, there lie dead
    One hundred twenty-six: added to these,
    Of knights, esquires, and gallant gentlemen,
    Eight thousand and four hundred; of which,
    Five hundred were but yesterday dubbed knights.
    So that, in these ten thousand they have lost,
    There are but sixteen hundred mercenaries;
    The rest are princes, barons, lords, knights, squires,
    And gentlemen of blood and quality.
    The names of those their nobles that lie dead:
    Charles Delabreth, High Constable of France,
    Jaques of Chatillon, Admiral of France,
    The Master of the Cross-bows, Lord Rambures,

Great Master of France, the brave Sir Guichard Dauphin,
John Duke of Alençon, Antony Duke of Brabant,
The brother to the Duke of Burgundy,
And Edward Duke of Bar: of lusty earls,
Grandpré and Roussi, Faulconbridge and Foix,
Beaumont and Marle, Vaudemont and Lestrake.
Here was a royal fellowship of death!
Where is the number of our English dead?

The Herald gives him another paper

Edward the Duke of York, the Earl of Suffolk,
Sir Richard Chichele, Davy Gam, esquire;
None else of name; and of all other men
But five-and-twenty. O God, your arm was here!
And not to us, but to your arm alone,
Ascribe we all! When, without stratagem,
But in plain shock and even play of battle,
Was ever known so great and little loss
On one part and on the other? Take it, God,
For it is only yours.

EXETER   But wonderful!

KING HENRY

Come, go we in procession to the village:
And be it death proclaimèd through our host
To boast of this, or take that praise from God
Which is his only.

FLUELLEN   Is it not lawful, please your majesty, to tell
how many is killed?

KING HENRY

Yes, Captain, but with this acknowledgement,
That God fought for us.

FLUELLEN Yes, my conscience, he did us great good.

KING HENRY

Do we all holy rites:
Let there be sung *Non Nobis* and *Te Deum,*

The dead with charity enclosed in clay;
And then to Calais, and to England then,
Where never from France arrived more happy men.

Exeunt

Prologue to Act V

Flourish. Enter Chorus

CHORUS

Now grant to those that have not read the story
That I may prompt them; and of such as have,
I humbly pray them to admit the excuse
Of time, of numbers, and due course of things,
Which cannot in their huge and proper life
Be here presented. Now we bear the King
Toward Calais. Grant him there: there seen,
Heave him away upon your wingèd thoughts
Athwart the sea. Behold, the English beach
Pales in the flood with men, with wives, and boys,
Whose shouts and claps outvoice the deep-mouthed sea,
Which like a mighty herald before the King
Seems to prepare his way. So let him land,
And solemnly see him set on to London.
So swift a pace has thought that even now
You may imagine him upon Blackheath,
Where now his lords desire him to have borne
His bruisèd helmet and his bended sword
Before him through the city. He forbids it,
Being free from vainness and self-glorious pride,
Giving full trophy, signal, and ostent
Quite from himself to God. But now behold,
In the quick forge and working-house of thought,
How London does pour out her citizens:
The Mayor and all his brethren in best sort,
Like the senators of the antique Rome,
With the plebeians swarmìng at their heels,
Go forth and fetch their conquering Caesar in.

As, by a lower but loving likelihood,
Were now the General of our gracious Empress—
As in good time he may—from Ireland coming,
Bringing rebellion spitted on his sword,
How many would the peaceful city quit
To welcome him! Much more, and much more cause,
Did they this Harry. Now in London place him—
As yet the lamentation of the French
Invites the King of England's stay at home.
The Emperor's coming in behalf of France
To order peace between them; and omit
All the occurrences, whatever chanced,
Till Harry's back-return again to France.
There must we bring him; and myself have played
The interim, by remembering you 'tis past.
Then brook abridgement, and your eyes advance,
After your thoughts, straight back again to France.

Exit

Act V

SCENE I
The English camp.

Enter Fluellen and Gower

GOWER   Nay, that's right; but why wear you your leek
today? Saint Davy's day is past.

FLUELLEN   There is occasion and cause why and wherefore
in all things. I will tell you as my friend, Captain
Gower: the rascally, scurvy, beggarly, lousy, bragging
knave Pistol—which you and yourself and all the world
know to be no better than a fellow, look you now, of no
merit—he is come to me and brings me bread and salt
yesterday, look you, and bid me eat my leek. It was in a
place where I could not breed contention with him; but
I will be so bold as to wear it in my cap till I see him
once again, and then I will tell him a little piece of my
desire.

Enter Pistol

GOWER   Why, here he comes, swelling like a turkey-cock.

FLUELLEN   'Tis no matter for his swelling nor his turkey-
cock. God bless you, Ancient Pistol! you scurvy, lousy
knave, God bless you!

PISTOL
Ha, are you bedlam? Do you thirst, base Troyan,
To have me fold up Parca's fatal web?
Hence! I am qualmish at the smell of leek.

FLUELLEN   I beseech you heartily, scurvy, lousy knave, at
    my desire, and my request, and my petition, to eat, look
    you, this leek. Because, look you, you do not love it, nor
    your affection, and your appetite, and your digestion,
    does not agree with it, I would desire you to eat it.

PISTOL
    Not for Cadwallader and all his goats!

FLUELLEN   There is one goat for you. (*He strikes him*)
    Will you be so good, scurvy knave, as eat it?

PISTOL
    Base Troyan, you shall die!

FLUELLEN   You say very true, scurvy knave, when God's
    will is. I will desire you to live in the meantime, and eat
    your victuals—come, there is sauce for it. (*He strikes
    him again*) You called me yesterday mountain-squire,
    but I will make you today a squire of low degree. I pray
    you fall to—if you can mock a leek, you can eat a leek.

GOWER   Enough, Captain, you have astonished him.

FLUELLEN   I say, I will make him eat some part of my
    leek, or I will beat his pate four days. Bite, I pray you, it
    is good for your green wound and your bloody coxcomb.

PISTOL   Must I bite?

FLUELLEN   Yes, certainly, and out of doubt, and out of
    question too, and ambiguity.

PISTOL   By this leek, I will most horribly revenge—I eat
    and eat, I swear—

FLUELLEN   Eat, I pray you; will you have some more
    sauce to your leek? There is not enough leek to swear by.

PISTOL   Quiet your cudgel, you do see I eat.

FLUELLEN   Much good do you, scurvy knave, heartily.
    Nay, pray you throw none away, the skin is good for
    your broken coxcomb. When you take occasion to see
    leeks hereafter, I pray you mock at them, that is all.

PISTOL   Good!

FLUELLEN   Ay, leeks are good. Hold you, there is a groat
    to heal your pate.

PISTOL   Me a groat?

FLUELLEN   Yes, verily and in truth you shall take it, or I
    have another leek in my pocket which you shall eat.

PISTOL   I take your groat in earnest of revenge.

FLUELLEN   If I owe you anything, I will pay you in
    cudgels—you shall be a woodmonger, and buy nothing
    of me but cudgels. Good-bye to you, and keep you, and
    heal your pate.   *Exit*

PISTOL

    All hell shall stir for this!

GOWER   Go, go, you are a counterfeit cowardly knave.
    Will you mock at an ancient tradition, begun upon an
    honourable respect, and worn as a memorable trophy of
    predeceased valour, and dare not make good in your
    deeds any of your words? I have seen you mocking and
    jeering at this gentleman twice or thrice. You thought,
    because he could not speak English in the native garb,
    he could not therefore handle an English cudgel. You
    find it otherwise, and henceforth let a Welsh correction
    teach you a good English disposition. Fare you well. *Exit*

PISTOL

    Does Fortune play the housewife with me now?
    News have I that my Nell is dead in hospital
    Of malady of France,
    And there my rendezvous is quite cut off.
    Old I do wax, and from my weary limbs
    Honour is cudgellèd. Well, bawd I'll turn,
    And something lean to cutpurse of quick hand.
    To England will I steal, and there I'll—steal;
    And patches will I get unto these cudgelled scars,
    And swear I got them in the Gallia wars.

                                                            Exit

SCENE II
France. The King's palace.

*Enter, at one door, King Henry, Exeter, Bedford, Gloucester,
Clarence, Warwick, Westmorland, Huntingdon, and
other Lords; at another, the French King, Queen
Isabel, the Princess Katherine, Alice,
and other French; the Duke of Burgundy
and his train*

KING HENRY

    Peace to this meeting, wherefor we are met!
    Unto our brother France, and to our sister,
    Health and fair time of day. Joy and good wishes
    To our most fair and princely cousin Katherine.
    And, as a branch and member of this royalty,
    By whom this great assembly is contrived,
    We do salute you, Duke of Burgundy;
    And, Princes French, and peers, health to you all!

FRENCH KING

    Right joyous are we to behold your face,
    Most worthy brother England: fairly met!
    So are you, Princes English, every one.

QUEEN ISABEL

    So happy be the issue, brother England,
    Of this good day, and of this gracious meeting,
    As we are now glad to behold your eyes—
    Your eyes which hitherto have borne in them,
    Against the French that met them in their bent,
    The fatal balls of murdering basilisks.
    The venom of such looks, we fairly hope,
    Have lost their quality, and that this day
    Shall change all griefs and quarrels into love.

KING HENRY

    To cry 'Amen' to that, thus we appear.

QUEEN ISABEL
    You English Princes all, I do salute you.
BURGUNDY
    My duty to you both, on equal love,
    Great Kings of France and England! That I have laboured
    With all my wits, my pains, and strong endeavours,
    To bring your most imperial majesties
    Unto this bar and royal interview,
    Your mightiness on both parts best can witness.
    Since, then, my office has so far prevailed
    That face to face, and royal eye to eye,
    You have now greeted, let it not disgrace me
    If I demand, before this royal view,
    What rub or what impediment there is
    Why the naked, poor, and mangled peace—
    Dear nurse of arts, plenties, and joyful births—
    Should not in this best garden of the world,
    Our fertile France, put up her lovely visage?
    Alas, she has from France too long been chased,
    And all her husbandry does lie on heaps,
    Corrupting in its own fertility.
    Her vine, the merry cheerer of the heart,
    Unprunèd dies; her hedges even-pleached,
    Like prisoners wildly overgrown with hair,
    Put forth disordered twigs; her fallow leas
    The darnel, hemlock, and rank fumitory
    Do root upon; while the coulter rusts
    That should deracinate such savagery.
    The even mead, that erst brought sweetly forth
    The freckled cowslip, burnet, and green clover,
    Wanting the scythe, all uncorrected, rank,
    Conceives by idleness, and nothing breeds
    But hateful docks, rough thistles, hemlocks, burs,
    Losing both beauty and utility.
    And as our vineyards, fallows, meads, and hedges,
    Defective in their natures, grow to wildness,

Even so our houses and ourselves and children
Have lost, or do not learn for want of time,
The sciences that should become our country;
But grow like savages—as soldiers will
That nothing do but meditate on blood—
To swearing and stern looks, diffused attire,
And everything that seems unnatural.
Which to reduce into our former favour
You are assembled; and my speech entreats
That I may know the bar why gentle peace
Should not expel these inconveniences,
And bless us with her former qualities.

KING HENRY
If, Duke of Burgundy, you would the peace
Whose want gives growth to imperfectiòns
Which you have cited, you must buy that peace
With full accord to all our just demands,
Whose tenors and particular effects
You have, enscheduled briefly, in your hands.

BURGUNDY
The King has heard them, though to them as yet
There is no answer made.

KING HENRY   Well then, the peace
Which you before so urged lies in his answer.

FRENCH KING
I have but with a cursory eye
O'erglanced the articles. Please it as yet your grace
To appoint some of your Council presently
To sit with us once more, with better heed
To re-survey them, we will suddenly
Pass our accept and pèremptory answer.

KING HENRY
Brother, we shall. Go, uncle Exeter,
And brother Clarence, and you, brother Gloucester,
Warwick, and Huntingdon, go with the King.
And take with you free power to ratify,

    Augment, or alter, as your wisdoms best
    Shall see advantageable for our dignity,
    Anything in or out of our demands,
    And we'll agree thereto. Will you, fair sister,
    Go with the Princes, or stay here with us?

QUEEN ISABEL
    Our gracious brother, I will go with them.
    Haply a woman's voice may do some good,
    When articles too nicely are insisted on.

KING HENRY
    Yet leave our cousin Katherine here with us;
    She is our capital demand, comprised
    Within the fore-rank of our articles.

QUEEN ISABEL
    She has good leave.
              Exeunt all but Henry, Katherine, and Alice

KING HENRY   Fair Katherine, and most fair,
    Will you please deign to teach a soldier terms
    Such as will enter at a lady's ear
    And plead his love-suit to her gentle heart?

KATHERINE   Your majesty shall mock at me; I cannot
speak your English.

KING HENRY   O fair Katherine, if you will love me soundly
with your French heart, I will be glad to hear you
confess it brokenly with your English tongue. Do you
like me, Kate?

KATHERINE   *Pardonnez-moi*, I cannot tell what is 'like
me'.

KING HENRY   An angel is like you, Kate, and you are like
an angel.

KATHERINE   *Que dit-il? que je suis semblable à les
anges?*[1]

---

[1]What does he say? That I am like the angels? Thus truly,
saving your grace, he says.

ALICE   *Oui, vraiment, sauf votre grâce, ainsi dit-il.*

KING HENRY   I said so, dear Katherine, and I must not
blush to affirm it.

KATHERINE   *O bon Dieu! Les langues des hommes sont
pleines de tromperies.*

KING HENRY   What says she, fair one? that the tongues of
men are full of deceits?

ALICE   *Oui,* that the tongues of men are full of deceits—
that is the *Princesse.*

KING HENRY   The Princess is the better Englishwoman.
In faith, Kate, my wooing is fit for your understanding.
I am glad you can speak no better English; for if you
could, you would find me such a plain king that you
would think I had sold my farm to buy my crown. I
know no ways to mince it in love, but directly to say, 'I
love you': then if you urge me farther than to say, 'Do
you, in faith?' I wear out my suit. Give me your answer,
in faith, do; and so clap hands, and a bargain. How say
you, lady?

KATHERINE   *Sauf votre honneur* [saving your honour]
I understand well.

KING HENRY   Well, if you would put me to verses, or to
dance for your sake, Kate, why, you undo me. For the
one, I have neither words nor measure; and for the
other, I have no strength in measure, yet a reasonable
measure in strength. If I could win a lady at leapfrog, or
by vaulting into my saddle with my armour on my
back, under the correction of bragging be it spoken, I
should quickly leap into a wife. Or if I might buffet for
my love, or bound my horse for her favours, I could lay
on like a butcher, and sit like a jackanapes, never off.
But, before God, Kate, I cannot look callow, nor gasp out

my eloquence, nor I have cunning in protestation: only downright oaths, which I never use till urged, nor ever break for urging. If you can love a fellow of this temper, Kate, whose face is not worth sunburning, that never looks in his glass for love of anything he sees there, let your eye be your cook. I speak to you plain soldier. If you can love me for this, take me; if not, to say to you that I shall die is true—but for your love, by the Lord, no—yet I love you too. And while you live, dear Kate, take a fellow of plain and uncoined constancy; for he perforce must do you right, because he has not the gift to woo in other places. For these fellows of infinite tongue, that can rhyme themselves into ladies' favours, they do always reason themselves out again. What! A speaker is but a prater, a rhyme is but a ballad. A good leg will fall; a straight back will stoop; a black beard will turn white; a curled pate will grow bald; a fair face will wither; a full eye will wax hollow. But a good heart, Kate, is the sun and the moon—or rather, the sun, and not the moon; for it shines bright and never changes, but keeps its course truly. If you would have such a one, take me; and take me, take a soldier; take a soldier, take a king. And what say you then to my love? Speak, my fair, and fairly, I pray you.

KATHERINE   Is it possible that I should love the *ennemi* of *France?*

KING HENRY   No, it is not possible you should love the enemy of France, Kate; but in loving me you should love the friend of France. For I love France so well that I will not part with a village of it—I will have it all mine: and Kate, when France is mine, and I am yours, then yours is France, and you are mine.

KATHERINE   I cannot tell what is that.

KING HENRY   No, Kate? I will tell you in French, which I am sure will hang upon my tongue like a new-married wife about her husband's neck, hardly to be shaken off.

*Je—quand sur la possession de France, et quand vous
avez la possession de moi,*—let me see, what then? Saint
Denis be my speed!—*donc vôtre est France, et vous êtes
mienne.*[2] It is as easy for me, Kate, to conquer the
kingdom as to speak so much more French. I shall never
move you in French, unless it be to laugh at me.

KATHERINE   *Sauf votre honneur, le français que vous
parlez, il est meilleur que l'anglais lequel je parle.*[3]

KING HENRY   No, faith, it is not, Kate; but your speaking
of my tongue, and I yours, most truly-falsely, must
needs be granted to be much at one. But Kate, do you
understand thus much English—can you love me?

KATHERINE   I cannot tell.

KING HENRY   Can any of your neighbours tell, Kate? I'll
ask them. Come, I know you love me; and at night,
when you come into your closet, you'll question this
gentlewoman about me. And I know, Kate, you will to
her dispraise those parts in me that you love with your
heart. But, good Kate, mock me mercifully; the rather,
gentle Princess, because I love you cruelly. If ever you
are mine, Kate, as I have a saving faith within me tells
me you shall, I get you by fighting, and you must
therefore needs prove a good soldier-breeder. Shall not
you and I, between Saint Denis and Saint George,
compound a boy, half French, half English, that shall
go to Constantinople and take the Turk by the beard?
Shall we not? What say you, my fair flower-de-luce?

KATHERINE   I do not know that.

KING HENRY   No, it is hereafter to know, but now to
promise. Do but now promise, Kate, you will endeavour
for your French part of such a boy, and for my English

----

[2]When, on possession of France and you have possession
of me, then France is yours and you are mine.
[3]Saving your honour, the French that you speak is better
than the English that I speak.

moiety take the word of a king and a bachelor. How answer you, *la plus belle Katherine du monde, mon très cher et devin déesse?*[4]

KATHERINE   Your majesty has *fausse* [false] French enough to deceive the most *sage demoiselle* [wise girl] that is *en France.*

KING HENRY   Now fie upon my false French! By my honour, in true English, I love you, Kate. By which honour I dare not swear you love me, yet my blood begins to flatter me that you do, notwithstanding the poor and untempering effect of my visage. Now blast my father's ambition! He was thinking of civil wars when he got me; therefore was I created with a stubborn outside, with an aspect of iron, that when I come to woo ladies I frighten them. But in faith, Kate, the older I wax, the better I shall appear. My comfort is that old age, that ill layer-up of beauty, can do no more spoil upon my face. You have me, if you have me, at the worst; and you shall find me, if you have me, better and better; and therefore tell me, most fair Katherine, will you have me? Put off your maiden blushes, confirm the thoughts of your heart with the looks of an empress, take me by the hand, and say, 'Harry of England, I am yours. Which word you shall no sooner bless my ear with but I will tell you aloud, 'England is yours, Ireland is yours, France is yours, and Henry Plantagenet is yours,' Though I speak it before his face, if he is not fellow with the best king, you shall find the best king of good fellows. Come, your answer in broken music—for your voice is music, and your English broken. Therefore, Queen of all, Katherine, break your mind to me in broken English—will you have me?

---

[4]The most lovely Katherine in the world, my dear and divine goddess.

KATHERINE   That is as it shall please the *Roi mon père.*
[King my father.]

KING HENRY   Nay, it will please him well, Kate—it shall
please him, Kate.

KATHERINE   Then it shall also content me.

KING HENRY   Upon that I kiss your hand, and I call you
my Queen.

KATHERINE   *Laissez, mon seigneur, laissez, laissez! Ma
foi, je ne veux point que vous abaissiez votre grandeur
en baisant la main d'une—notre Seigneur—indigne
serviteur. Excusez-moi, je vous supplie, mon très puissant
seigneur.* [5]

KING HENRY   Then I will kiss your lips, Kate.

KATHERINE   *Les dames et demoiselles pour être baisées
devant leurs noces, il n'est pas la coûtume de France.*

KING HENRY   Madam my interpreter, what says she?

ALICE   That it is not the fashion *pour les* ladies of *France*—I
cannot tell what is *baiser en* Anglish.

KING HENRY   To kiss.

ALICE   Your majesty *entend* better *que moi.* [understands
better than I.]

KING HENRY   It is not a fashion for the maids in France to
kiss before they are married, would she say?

ALICE   *Oui, vraiment.* [Yes, truly.]

KING HENRY   O Kate, nice customs curtsy to great kings.
Dear Kate, you and I cannot be confined within the
weak list of a country's fashion. We are the makers of
manners, Kate, and the liberty that follows our places
stops the mouth of all find-faults. As I will do yours for
upholding the nice fashion of your country in denying
me a kiss; therefore, patiently, and yielding. (*He kisses
her*) You have witchcraft in your lips, Kate: there is
more eloquence in a sugar touch of them than in the
tongues of the French Council, and they should sooner

---

[5]Let be, my lord. Faith, I do not wish you to lower your
greatness by kissing the hand of an unworthy servitor.

persuade Harry of England than a general petition of monarchs. Here comes your father.

Enter the French King and Queen, Burgundy, and English and French Lords

BURGUNDY   God save your majesty! My royal cousin, teach you our Princess English?

KING HENRY   I would have her learn, my fair cousin, how perfectly I love her, and that is good English.

BURGUNDY   Is she not apt?

KING HENRY   Our tongue is rough, cousin, and my condition is not smooth; so that, having neither the voice nor the heart of flattery about me, I cannot so conjure up the spirit of love in her that it will appear in its true likeness.

BURGUNDY   Pardon the frankness of my mirth, if I answer you for that. If you would conjure in her, you must make a circle; if conjure up love in her in its true likeness, it must appear naked and blind. Can you blame her, then, being a maid yet rosed over with the virgin crimson of modesty, if she denies the appearance of a naked blind boy in her naked seeing self? It is, my lord, a hard condition for a maid to consent to.

KING HENRY   Yet they do wink and yield, as love is blind and enforces.

BURGUNDY   They are then excused, my lord, when they see not what they do.

KING HENRY   Then, good my lord, teach your cousin to consent winking.

BURGUNDY   I will wink on her to consent, my lord, if you will teach her to know my meaning: for maids, well summered and warm kept, are like flies at Bartholomewtide, blind, though they have their eyes. And then they will endure handling, which before would not abide looking on.

KING HENRY   This moral ties me over to time and a hot
    summer; and so I shall catch the fly, your cousin, in the
    latter end, and she must be blind too.

BURGUNDY   As love is, my lord, before it loves.

KING HENRY   It is so; and you may, some of you, thank
    love for my blindness, who cannot see many a fair
    French city for one fair French maid that stands in my
    way.

FRENCH KING   Yes, my lord, you see them perspectively,
    the cities turned into a maid; for they are all girdled
    with maiden walls, that war has never entered.

KING HENRY   Shall Kate be my wife?

FRENCH KING   So please you.

KING HENRY   I am content, so the maiden cities you talk
    of may wait on her: so the maid that stood in the way for
    my wish shall show me the way to my will.

FRENCH KING
    We have consented to all terms of reason.

KING HENRY
    Is it so, my lords of England?

WESTMORLAND
    The King has granted every article:
    His daughter first, and then, in sequel, all,
    According to their firm proposèd natures.

EXETER
    Only he has not yet subscribèd this:
    Where your majesty demands that the King of France,
    having any occasion to write for matter of grant,
    shall name your highness in this form, and with this
    addition, in French, *Notre très cher fils Henri, Roi
    d'Angleterre, Héritier de France:* and thus in Latin,
    *Praeclarissimus filius noster Henricus, Rex Angliae
    et Haeres Franciae.*[6]

---

[6]Our dearest son, Henry, King of England, Heir of France.

FRENCH KING

   And this I have not, brother, so denied

   But your request shall make me let it pass.

KING HENRY

   I pray you then, in love and dear alliance,

   Let that one article rank with the rest,

   And thereupon give me your daughter.

FRENCH KING

   Take her, fair son, and from her blood raise up

   Issue to me, that the contending kingdoms

   Of France and England, whose very shores look pale

   With envy of each other's happiness,

   May cease their hatred; and this dear conjunction

   Plant neighbourhood and Christian-like accord

   In their sweet bosoms, that never war advance

   His bleeding sword between England and fair France.

LORDS   Amen!

KING HENRY

   Now welcome, Kate; and bear me witness all

   That here I kiss her as my sovereign Queen.

Flourish

QUEEN ISABEL

   God, the best maker of all marriages,

   Combine your hearts in one, your realms in one!

   As man and wife, being two, are one in love,

   So be there between your kingdoms such a spousal

   That never may ill office, or mad jealousy,

   Which troubles oft the bed of blessèd marriage,

   Thrust in between the compact of these kingdoms

   To make divorce of their incorporate league;

   That English may as French, French Englishmen,

   Receive each other, God speak this 'Amen'!

ALL   Amen!

KING HENRY

    Prepare we for our marriage; on which day,
    My Lord of Burgundy, we'll take your oath,
    And all the peers', for surety of our leagues.
    Then shall I swear to Kate, and you to me,
    And may our oaths well kept and prosperous be!

Sennet. Exeunt

Epilogue

❀

Enter Chorus

CHORUS
    Thus far, with rough and all-unable pen,
      Our bending author has pursued the story,
    In little room confining mighty men,
      Mangling by starts the full course of their glory.
    Small time, but in that small most greatly lived
      This star of England. Fortune made his sword,
    By which the world's best garden he achieved,
      And of it left his son imperial lord.
    Henry the Sixth, in infant bands crowned King
      Of France and England, did this King succeed,
    Whose state so many had the managing
      That they lost France, and made his England bleed:
    Which oft our stage has shown; and, for their sake,
      In your fair minds let this acceptance take.   *Exit*

Appendix to
Act III, Scene IV

Enter Princess Katherine and Alice, an old gentlewoman

KATHERINE   Alice, you have been in England, and you speak the language well.

ALICE   A little, madam.

KATHERINE   Pray, teach me—I must learn to speak it. How do you call *la main* in English?

ALICE   *La main?* It is called the hand.

KATHERINE   The hand. And *les doigts?*

ALICE   *Les doigts?* Faith, I forget *les doigts,* but I shall remember. I think that they are called the fingers; yes, the fingers.

KATHERINE   *La main,* the hand; *les doigts,* the fingers. I think I am a good pupil; I have learned two words of English quickly. How do you call *les ongles?*

ALICE   *Les ongles?* We call them the nails.

KATHERINE   The nails. Listen: tell me if I speak well— the hand, the fingers, and the nails.

ALICE   Well said, madam. It is very good English.

KATHERINE   Tell me the English for *le bras.*

ALICE   The arm, madam.

KATHERINE   And *le coude?*

ALICE   The elbow.

KATHERINE   The elbow. I will repeat all the words you have taught me up to this.

ALICE   That is too difficult, madam, as I think.

KATHERINE   Excuse me, Alice; listen—the hand, the fingers, the nails, the arm, the bilbow.

ALICE   The elbow, madam.

KATHERINE   O Lord, I forget! The elbow. How do you call *le col?*

ALICE   The neck, madam.

KATHERINE   The neck. And *le menton?*

ALICE   The chin.

KATHERINE   The chin. *Le col,* the neck; *le menton,* the chin.

ALICE   Yes. Saving your honour, truly, you pronounce the words as well as the natives of England.

KATHERINE   I don't doubt I shall learn, by God's grace, and in little time.

ALICE   You haven't already forgotten what I have taught you?

KATHERINE   No. I will recite to you at once: the hand, the finger, the mails.

ALICE   The nails, madam.

KATHERINE   The nails, the arm, the ilbow.

ALICE   Saving your honour, the elbow.

KATHERINE   So I say: the elbow, the neck, and the chin. How do you call *le pied* and *la robe?*

ALICE   The foot, madam, and the count. [gown]

KATHERINE   The foot, and the count? O Lord, they are bad words, unsuitable, gross, vulgar, not for ladies of honour to use. I wouldn't want to pronounce those words before the lords of France, for all the world. Foh! The foot and the count! Still, I will recite once more my lesson together: the hand, the finger, the nails, the arm, the neck, the chin, the foot, the count.

ALICE   Excellent, madam.

KATHERINE   It's enough for once. Let's go to dinner.

Exeunt